The Rosicrucian Ha... tic
Textbook of S...

The Original American Illuminati
Loge de Parfaits d' Écosse ™- 1764

Americas First Rosicrucian Rose Croix High Degrees and Initiations -Mystical Christian, Hermetic, Hellenistic, Buddhist, Brahmin, Persian, & Oriental Wisdom
By: Magus Incognito & George Mentz

"Before the Illuminati & Before the Skull and Bones was the Temple of the Lodge of Perfection in the New World"

Preface	6
Part I. - Loge de Parfaits 1764 - History, Doctrines and Tenets	8
The Philosophy and Origins of Masonic and Rosicrucian Organizations	13
Rosicrucian-Masonic Mysteries - 21st Century	14
The Rosicrucian Lodge of Perfection & the Original 25 Degree initiations from the 1750s.	16
9 Secret Principles and Grades and Degrees of the Celtic Rose Croix Master	19
Part II. The Teachings, Essays, Metaphysics and Secrets.	22
Laws of Attraction & Mental Attitude	22
Karma and Correspondences	24
Atonement and Purity of Mind	25
The Power of Prayer and Meditation	27
7 Cosmic Principles - Rosicrucian & Hermetic – The Kyballion Laws	30
Emerald Tablets	36
Desire and Purpose	37
Reincarnation, Reinvention, and Rebirth	41
The Leading Metaphysical Law	43
How the Mind Creates Your World and Character	45
How Mental Pictures Become Realities	48
The Seventh Aphorism of Rosicrucianism	51
Oriental Rosicrucian Success Principles with a Western Interpretation	53
Rosicrucians Americana - Virtues by: Benjamin Franklin	59
The Rose Croix & Rosicrucian Principles of Healing	60
Health & Healing Exercise	60
Rosicrucians and Mind Skills and Oriental Virtues	63
Rosicrucian Exercises	65
Concentration Exercise	65
Active Meditation Exercise for Intuition and Guidance	65
Exercise for Energizing or Healing Yourself.	66
Five Exercises to Augment Peace of Mind and Mental Abilities	67
Perception and Awareness Exercise	70
Affirmations and Exercises	71
List of affirmations to improve energy, peace, and confidence.	72
Twelve Meditations and Affirmations for Peace of Mind - Affirmations	74
Manifesting Your Dreams – An Exercise of Realization	77
Things to Remember about Co-Creating and Manifesting Your Life	79

Thoughts on Manifesting your Future and Increasing Faith	80
Personal Magnetism	82
Cycles of Life	87
Philosophy of Harmony and Gratitude	89
The Philosophy of Wealth	91
The Philosophy of Greatness	93
Harmony and Creation	94
Teachings and Strategies of Spiritual Growth	96
Rosy Cross Americana – A Summary of Effective Metaphysics	102
Tree of Life and The 9 Worlds	110
Buddhist Eight Fold Path to Happiness 四圣谛: - Indo-Aryan Thought	112
Summary of The Eightfold Path	118
Creative Success Executive Summary	119
More Metaphysical Issues & Insights	125
Initiation of Mastery Exercises in 28 Parts	136
24-28 - Module Twendy-Five Through Twenty Eight – Observations	155
The Elemental Mind and Body	158
Some Observations	159
Taoism	162
Chakras and Eastern Exercises	165
Native American Spirituality	167
Native American Spiritual Exercise:	169
The 12 Characteristics of Magical and Prosperous People	170
Rosicrucian Exercises with Magical Power	171
1. Basic Prayers for Memory	171
2. Fellowship Exercise	171
3. Active Meditation	172
4. Seeking Inspiration	172
5. Seeking God Consciousness	173
6. Mass as a Sacrament	173
7. Absorption Exercise:	173
8. Willingness Exercise:	174
9. Give It Away Exercise:	175
10. Character Building Ritual	176
11. Awareness Exercise:	177
12. Association Exercise:	177
13. Creativity:	177

14.	Spiritual Gymnasium	177
15.	Sacred Days	178
16.	Services and Sacred Space	178
17.	Nature Bound and Pilgrimages and Commitments	179
18.	Communing with Yourself	179
19.	Catharsis and Purification	180
20.	Contemplative Action	181
22.	Meditative Objects	182
23.	Spiritual Jewelry and Charms	183
24.	Energy Centers	183
25.	Higher Self Visitation Exercises	183
26.	Mantras	184
27.	Prayer for Others and Forgiveness	185
28.	Hospitality Exercise	185
29.	Celtic Action	185
30.	Sabbath	185
31.	Environmental Exercise	186
32.	Character Exercise	186
33.	Tithe Exercise	187

The Process of Magic and Manifesting 187

Part III. - Appendix - Confessio Fraternitatis R.C - AD Eruditos Europa 192

Appendix - The Fraternity of the Rose Cross & Masonic History 199

    The Historical Postulate of Rosicrucianism 201

Origins of The Ancient Esoteric Tradition - Earliest Indo-European Religions ... 208

    Some Core Historical Spiritual Practices and Beliefs of Mesopotamia 211

Babylonian "Counsels of Wisdom" 1500 B.C. 213

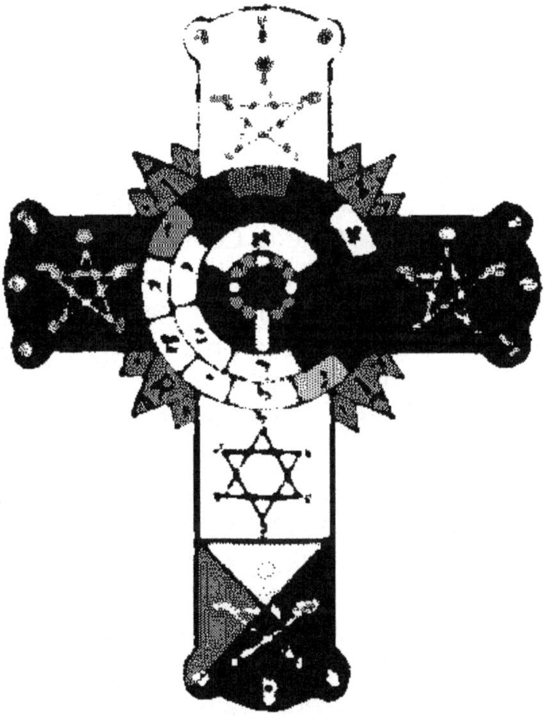

Preface

In writing this manuscript, it must be remembered that there were several esoteric traditions reemerging at the same time in Central Europe, England, Germany and France. The Manifestos of the Rosicrucians were the Fama Fraternitatis and the Confessio Fraternitatis. The Fama has wonderful stories of Christian Rosenkreutz i.e. Christian Rose Cross along with an emphasis on philosophy, science and medicine while the Confessio offers a statements of belief. See Appendix. These works were published in Latin in Cassel in 1615.

With both the Confessio and the Fama, there is a focus on individual spiritual growth for the first time in modern history in that the Fama's writings imply that, "a man should strive to better understand his own nobleness and worth"

In the midst of this spiritual and intellectual renaissance, several organizations of higher learning and mysticism were becoming public for the first time since the fall of Templarism on March 11, 1313. With this rebirth of the mystery teachings in the 1500s and 1600s, there is a noticeable influences between the: Masons, Rosicrucians, Hermeticism, Hellenism, New Templars, Teutonic Knights, Pietism, New-Platonic Thought, Mystical Christianity, Orientalism, Persian Mysticism, Theosophy, Practical Christianity, and other Holy Land teachings.

The author has given great thought as to how to add an English Language version of the major topics of interest of these groups for translation. Keep in mind that the primary Loge de Parfaits' languages of the 1760's were French, Dutch, and German. Much of this document is original writings and contributions of the author, some of these essays are updated versions of writings by 19th and 20th century Rosicrucians, Templars, & high ranking masons, while some is taken "word for word" from pre- 1925 authors who made the best analysis and contribution to any individual topic.

In the 1700s, New Orleans was one of the largest ports in what would become the USA. New Orleans was also home to most of the immigrants to the French and Spanish Territories in the 1700s and 1800s, and was unique at that time to many languages and cultures. This book is about the teachings and history of the Secret Lodge of 1764. This knowledge is updated and revitalized to provide a view of the original lessons and initiations from this clandestine lodge. Almost 250 years later, we can see how these secret teachings transcended the dogma of central Europe and allowed the member practitioner to become an ordained metaphysician of the highest levels. Even to this day, the State Flag of Louisiana and the real symbol of the Rosicrucians is that of a pelican tearing open its breast to feed its little ones -- the symbol of the 18th degree of the order.

Keep in mind that the Masonic Lodges as we know them did not need other degrees or higher initiations. However, in the early 1700s, German and French lodges began to create new mystical degrees or initiations of Noble and Scottish-Templar flair.

All Rights Reserved 2008-9 – No reproduction of this content in any way is allowed without the permission of the Author, Supreme Magus or the Board of the <u>Loge de Parfaits d'Escosse</u> ™

Part I. - Loge de Parfaits 1764 - History, Doctrines and Tenets

The Louisiane Territory was first claimed by French explorer de LaSalle in 1682, It was named Louisiane for King Louis X1V of France. This was 133 years after the Mississippi river had been first sighted by a European; a Spanish adventurer named de Soto. The old colonial city of New Orleans was founded in 1718 and by 1764 had grown to such importance that a group of Dutch, French, Spanish and Central Europeans founded the secret "Loge de Parfaits" or Lodge of Perfection which was the first organization in the Americas to offer the 25 higher initiations and degrees of Mysticism, Masonry and Rosicrucianism sometimes referred to as "The Rites of the Royal Secrets or Rose Croix" or Loge de Parfaits d' Écosse. Later in New Orleans, Hellenistic Oriental religious bodies, Italian Brotherhoods, African magical cults, and secret orders would be founded, such as the Mystic Greek Orthodox Church USA, the Italian Mafia, the Arts of African Voodoo, American Pagan Carnival, and Mardi Gras. In the city that allowed America to be finally freed from European domination at the Battle of New Orleans, a spiritual renaissance had flowered secretly under the influences of France, Spain and England, along with massive immigrations from Italy, Germany, Ireland and many other central European powers. The Louisiane Territory was purchased by the USA in 1803, but before this event, the mystical rites of the Secret Loge de Parfaits were already deeply established in New Orleans. To this day, New Orleans is rich in culture, mythology, and spirituality as evidenced in the secret krewes, clubs, and orders related to Mardi Gras and carnival. Some of the largest fraternal and societal cemeteries in the world are located in New Orleans. Below, we will examine some of the earlier influences on the Rosy Cross Philosophy and Brotherhoods which led to the Sovereign Body in the Americas. Throughout this book, the followers of the Rose Croix may be referred to as: The Brotherhood, The Society, The Fraternity, The Lodge, The Craft, or The Fellowship. "The Brothers of the Rosy Cross"

The modern interest in the Rosicrucian Teachings dates back to the early part of the seventeenth century--about 1610, to be exact. As we would anticipate, the mysteries and secret wisdom that had been around since before Cesar was now resurfacing during the era of Martin Luther,

Religious Change, and the Renaissance. During this period, there were rumors of the existence of a society known as "The Brothers of the Rosy Cross," the officers and meeting places of which were not known to the public. The mysterious society was severely attacked by the ecclesiastical authorities and others, and was as vigorously defended by those who were interested in the general subject of mysticism and the esoteric teachings. During the 1700's., many of the original teachings of the Rosicrucians have also existed within the higher degrees of Masonry. Thus, there is still curiosity about the cross pollination between them during the establishment and growth of both fellowships.   The legend concerning Esoteric Rosicrucianism is as follows: That a certain Christian Rosenkreutz, a German nobleman who had donned the robes of a certain order of monks, had visited India, Persia, and also Arabia, and had returned bringing with him a certain Secret Doctrine obtained from the sages and seers of those Oriental lands. He was said to have established the original Rosicrucian Brotherhood about 1425 in the German French Border Regions, its existence not becoming generally known until nearly two hundred years afterward.   * Furthermore, The Loge de Parfaits d' Écosse in New Orleans of 1764 was also based on the Lore of the Knights Templar or The Poor Fellow-Soldiers of Christ and of the Temple of Solomon who also had held the secret knowledge and faith of the Orient. The legend is that the Knights took refuge in Scotland and operated in a clandestine way until their resurgence as the Lodge of Perfection of Scotland. The present writer does not care to prove up the nexus of Rosicrucianism, templar wisdom and masonry because it has been in existence for over almost 250 years in the New World.

Regardless of your feelings and prior knowledge as to this order, the Secret Wisdom of the Rose Croix and Holy Knights is a body of mystic teachings, handed down for ages by wise men deeply versed in the esoteric doctrines and metaphysical truth. This Insights of the Rosy Cross originally came by way of Ancient Europe, The Middle East, Egypt & North Africa, and The Orient, and in fact, even today, comprises part of the Inner Teachings of some of the highest Oriental Brotherhoods. Its history is but another instance of the truth of the old Secret axioms, one of which says "The open hands can receive the treasure". For many years little or nothing was permitted to be revealed to the general public concerning the Secret Doctrine of the Rose Croix, but during the past one-hundred and twenty-five years there has been a greater, and still greater freedom in this respect, until today many important Rosicrucian rites, initiations, exercises, and teachings form a part of nearly all writings and teachings upon the subject of the Esotericism in general, and of the Higher Metaphysics in particular. Theosophy and Theophysics, and the general interest in Oriental Philosophies and Religions, have done much to bring into public notice some of the more elementary points of the Secret Rites and Degrees.

The Higher Alchemy

The Rosicrucians, according to the public encyclopedias, and other works of reference, are held to have been devoted to the subject of Alchemy. And, indeed, this statement is correct. But the modern compilers of such reference books have fallen into the error of supposing that the Alchemy referred to was performed wholly upon the Plane of Matter--and concerned wholly with the Transmutation of Elements. They are ignorant of the fact that the Alchemy which attracted the Rosicrucians, and which took up most of their time and attention, was Mental Alchemy, and Spiritual Transformation --something quite different indeed, though having of course a correspondence to the Material Alchemy, according to the Law of Cause and Effect. The student of the present book will discover this fact, and will receive many valuable hints concerning the higher forms of the wisdom teachings, providing he is prepared to read between the lines of the text, and to reason by Analogy. The axiom "As above, so below," will be found to work out well in this connection. TRUSTWORTHY information is unavailable concerning the actual philosophical beliefs, political aspirations, and humanitarian activities of the Rosicrucian Fraternity. Evidence points to the probable existence of several distinct Rosicrucian bodies: an inner organization whose members never revealed their identity or teachings to the world. However, in FREE America, the teachings were codified, taught, honed and actually practiced in allegory and in lecture to qualified men of substance. As said by the ancients, "Many are called but few are chosen." When Rosicrucianism became the philosophical school of the seventeenth century, numerous documents on the subject were also circulated for purely commercial purposes by impostors desirous of capitalizing its popularity. However, the degrees, rites, ceremonies and lessons of this ancient initiation have maintained their structure for hundreds of years.

Does the wisdom evolve? The answer is yes and no. Most historians and philosophers could argue that the tenets are new but relate them easily to the greatest minds of history. The teachings in this manuscript can be traced back to Aristotle, Hermetic Insights, Celtic & Druidic Mythology, Hellenistic, Romanic Thought, Pythagoras, Taoism, Zoroastrianism, Vedic Wisdom, Nordic Eddas, Mystics, Greco-Buddhism, and more. The process of including the wisdom that enhances life, joy, and prosperity, and courage cannot be ignored. Furthermore, with the wisdom of the East and the New Wisdom of the Native American Holy Shaman, eternal and global truths began to truly unfold in the New World for the very first time in history.

The Secrets of The Rose Croix Brotherhood had found initial refuge in the Palatinate or Rhine of Germany and also Strasbourg which is near the Northern French boarder in the 1500's. This was also a bastion of Lutheran, Calvinist and Free Celtic Catholic thinking and spiritual reform at the time. Dynamic religious thinking had begun to flourish under King Frederick V (Elector of Palatine of the Rhine) in the 1600s. Wars and battles over royal boundaries and Catholic Orthodoxy plagued the central European, Bavarian, and Rhineland regions for over 100 more years which caused a "Christian Holocaust" forcing huge emigrations out to the "*NeuLand*" or American Colonies. In Europe, Masonic and Rosicrucian activities had been in existence for some years and become more open since the liberations and philosophical-movements of Martin Luther and other revolutionaries. Moreover, a number of new, enhanced and mystical degree initiations had been established in Germany and France. Around 1744, a French trader, by the name of Estienne Morin became involved in Bordeaux chapter of Masonry in France. Around 1747, Morin became determined to found an "Ecossais" lodge (Scots Masters Lodge) in the new world. It is now generally accepted that this Rite of twenty-five "haut or hautes" or high degrees was compiled by Estienne Morin with help from Henry Francken, and these lessons are today titled "The Rites of the Royal Secret".

The one man who was most important in assisting Morin in spreading the degrees in the New World was a naturalized French subject of Dutch origin named Henry Andrew Francken. Francken worked closely with Morin to produced a manuscript book giving the rituals for the 4th through the 25th degrees. During this time, The Les Loge de Parfaits d' Écosse was formed in 1763 and established on 12 April 1764 at New Orleans, becoming the first high degree lodge on the North American continent. Its public life, however, was short, because the Treaty of Paris (1763) ceded New Orleans from France to Spain, and the Catholic Spanish crown had been historically hostile to Freemasonry. Soon thereafter, Francken travelled to New York in 1767 where he granted a 2nd Patent, dated 26 December 1767, for the formation of a Lodge of Perfection at Albany. This marked the first time the Degrees of Perfection (the 4th through the 14th) were conferred in one of the thirteen British colonies.   Although the New Orleans Chapter of Perfection and Royal Secrets remained clandestine, it never died. This book addresses the philosophies and teachings of the Secret Lodge as delivered by its' Supreme Magus.   The fundamental symbols of the Rosicrucians were the rose and the cross; the rose female and the cross male, both universal phallic emblems. We observe that the rose and the cross typify the generative and constructive processes, but we must be able to pierce the veil of symbolism; and realize that the creative mystery in the material world is merely a shadow of the divine creative mystery in the spiritual world.

While it is quite true that the alchemical retort symbolizes the creation, it also has a far more significant meaning concealed under the allegory of the second birth. As regeneration is the key to spiritual existence, they therefore founded their symbolism upon the rose and the cross, which typify the redemption and transmutation of man through the union of his lower temporal nature with his higher eternal nature. The rosy cross is also a hieroglyphic figure representing the formula of the Universal Medicine. [i] The rose is also an Egyptian symbol of rebirth; an attribute of the Hindu Prosperity goddess Lakshmi; and a part of the Rosalia festivals associated with Dionysus who was an important patron of the mysteries of Eleusis.[ii]

The Philosophy and Origins of Masonic and Rosicrucian Organizations

One need only to read Aristotle and contemplate the Law of Correspondences or laws of "cause and effect" to see the influences of the great thinkers of Socrates and Plato that exist in today's teachings in the mystical lodges and metaphysical societies of the world. Read the meditations of Marcus Aurelius to capture the essences of the great virtues of the mighty pre-Christian warriors and emperors. To seek more light, read the works of Meister Eckhart, Hegel, Shopenhauer, Descartes, and Swedenborg to comprehend their views of creative intelligence, power, and prayer.

The essays and topics covered in this manuscript did not come into being from a vacuum. The teachings of the ancient Babylonians, Assyrians, Mesopotamians, and Egyptians are clear influences. The mysteries of the Ancient Persians, Greeks and Italians are also peppered throughout these pages. It could be said that many of the teachings included have been gathered from Pythagoras, Hermes, Plato, Amenhotep/Akhnaton, the Essenes, and the Great Nazarene Master. From the beginnings of time, seekers have tried to cultivate their soul and latent powers along with improving their peace of mind and connection to the spirit world. Much of this book is devoted to the mysteries that would allow for spiritual growth in any person who seeks greater light.

From a historical perspective, the initiations, secrets, and lessons in this book were the beginnings of "free thinking esoteric and mystical philosophy" in the new world. These higher teachings were the first of their kind that were occurring in a place that was the first melting pot in the New World "NEW ORLEANS". Today, the consistory lodges of perfection around the world still adhere to a somewhat similar structure as in 1764 in the New Colony of New Orleans. The first three degrees are what brings a man into young adulthood as a mason, builder or creator. After that, the higher degrees instilled wisdom, courage, insights, mysteries, and peace. These higher rites are the 1) 4° through 14°- Lodge of Perfection 2) Parts of 15° through 28° Degrees are the Council of

Holy Knights and Kadosh or Prince of Jerusalem 3) Parts of Degrees 15° through 28° are Chapter of the Rose Croix. Later, in the 1800's, the new and enhanced list of supplemental or consistory degrees going up to the 32° degree and 33° degree HONORS were being used around the world. Keep in mind that the bulk of the original membership of this higher European fellowship were Roman Catholics from Southwest Germany and Northern France. Because the new rites of perfection and Loge de Parfaits was beyond Masonry, any Papal Bull did not apply to the higher degrees that were originally Judeo-Christian. These essays or rites are steps to improving ones mental, spiritual and physical life. Heed the teachings in this book to master a greater path. The strategies and lessons herein are the higher mysteries that can propel the initiate into the 4th dimension of existence on this Earth.

Rosicrucian-Masonic Mysteries - 21st Century

The Rosicrucian's [Orders and Societies of the Rosy Cross or Rose Croix] study the teachings of the ancient masters, mysteries, and prophets along with the world's most effective wisdom. The Masonic Rose Croix and The Orders of Rosicruciana/Rose Cross philosophies attempt to gather and harvest the most valuable, mystical, and "life expanding" philosophies that can allow individuals to grow on a spiritual and mental level. Orthodox Rosicrucians tend to focus more on Hermetic, Egyptian, Vedic and Taoist philosophical aspects of metaphysics, alchemy, reincarnation and evolution. The Rose Croix Masonic Degrees also contained the Orthodox Rosicrucianism but also encompass the Hellenistic, Roman, Celtic, Nordic, and Holy Land Rites. Both traditional Rosicrucians and Masonic Rose Croix initiations degrees and orders have been well organized for hundreds or even thousands of years, and both have educated multitudes of people on varying aspects of spiritual and philosophical wisdom as well as teaching methods on how to obtain enlightenment and inner personal growth. Masonry places great emphasis on "character building" and "teaching by allegory" which means bringing people together to give lessons almost in the form of an enacted skit or play to see and feel the actual lesson taught. [iii] Traditional Rosicrucian and Masonic teachings also include many mental exercises and for the practitioner.

Some core beliefs or practices would be:

- To facilitate the awareness of harmony with the Supreme and to expel the mental separateness from God.
- All people have great potential and latent powers. The teachings allow each participant to grow and tap into greater mental and spiritual abilities.
- To improve the character of all members so that they may better serve society and humanity.
- God is an impersonal Supreme Intelligence. Masons generally refer to God as the Supreme Architect or Creator.
- Rosicrucians teach more information about life cycles what some would consider ancient methods of astrology and also believe in the general evolution of man's mind, body and spirit using a "Law of Sevens". Masons also believe in the cycles of personal growth and development of people but it is more devoted to grades of development as compared to "periods in you individual life path".
- Masons and Rosicrucians believe that all people have the right to a direct experience of profound attunement with the Supreme Intelligence. Therefore, each person has the right to spiritual harmony and a personal relationship with The God of their understanding.
- Great reverence to all religions and their sacred scripture.

*The Loge de Parfaits d' Écosse in New Orleans of 1764 was based on the Lore of the Knights Templar or The **Poor Fellow-Soldiers of Christ and of the Temple of Solomon. The legend is that the**

Knights took refuge in Scotland and operated in a clandestine way until their resurgence as the Lodge of Perfection of Scotland.

The Rosicrucian Lodge of Perfection & the Original 25 Degree initiations from the 1750s.

These numbered initiations are each a lesson. Imagine each number being a college course or seminar. The lesson or eternal truths of each degree below are reenacted by a group of people in a small allegoric play of sorts. Thus, the individual sees and feels the lesson regarding each teaching. The First Three Degrees are the Apprentice, Fellowcraft and Maaster.

1° Entered Apprentice - Truth is a divine attribute and the foundation of every virtue.
Lesson: Teachings on the four cardinal virtues of: Fortitude, Prudence, Temperance and Justice
2° Degree FellowCraft - To relieve the distressed is a duty incumbent on all men..
Lesson: Truly commendable virtues of Brotherly Love, Relief and Truth
3° Master Mason - Learning to be your best and enjoy a well spent life
Lesson: Virtue of Fidelity and Awareness. Among masons, there is no higher rank than that of Master Mason.in the Masonic Fraternity. The rest of these degrees are to seek more light.
4 ° Secret Master – Duty to the Supreme, family and country.
Lessson: Duty is the essence of this degree. Being open to lead and to follow good examples.
5 ° Perfect Master - honesty and trustworthiness is the cornerstone.
Lesson: Live your life well and to you best.
6 ° Intimate Secretary - duty, charity, toleration & development of an accurate view of self, society, and world. Becoming Non-Defensive.
Lesson: Be a zealous and faithful person while acting as a peacemaker. Be Mindful of others.

7 ° Provost and Judge - Judge with patience and impartially.   Non-Judgment
Lesson: Let equity and justice of your heart be your guide

8 ° The Intendant of the building - charity, morality and kindness.
Lesson: If you take care of your temple, you will be better equipped to help others.

9 ° Masters of the Temple of 9 - Candor and generosity. Self Acceptance and acceptance of nature.
Lesson: Enlighten your soul and mind and in turn, help to educate others.

10 ° Master Elected of 15 - Freedoms of political and spiritual ideologies should be shared by all.
Lesson: Develop a command of speech in thought, word and deed.

11 ° Sublime Master Selected - Compassionate to brothers and to all mankind. Being Authentic combined with having boldness and spontaneity.
Lesson: Being Contemplative in Action.

12 ° Great Masters Architect - Faith in morality and virtue and in God. "Life is what each man makes of it." Being creative and solution oriented where possible
Lesson: Learn to meditate and be aware of the opportunities and ideas in life.

13 ° Master Royal Arch - Liberty; in our mind and our hearts. A sense of Mission and Purpose
Lesson: Learning to be bold and engage right efforts and directing of energies.

14 ° Grand Elect Mason – Self Analysis and Prayer/Meditation; Reflection and detachment.
Lesson: Developing a Right Understanding is Key to Growth.

15 ° Rose Croix Degree - Knight of Sword - Fidelity to obligations and perseverance of purpose under difficulties. Selfless service to the Family, Group and Community.
Lesson: Integrity and honesty will command respect from all.

16 ° **Rose Croix Degree** - Prince of Jerusalem - nobility of self-sacrifice and Patience

17 ° **Rose Croix Degree** - Knight of East and West – Loyalty to the Supreme is the primary obligation.
Lesson: Maintaining a thankful heart, appreciative attitude in general.

18 ° **Rose Croix Degree** - Knight of the White Eagle or Pelican – Also Knight of St. Andrew. Life and its strength come from God. The rose signifies the dawn and the cross is a sacred symbol of antiquity in many cultures. Symbols: The Rose, Golden Cross, Pelican and Eagle. **Duties**: Practice virtue. Rightly engage labor and avoid vice. Be tolerant of the beliefs of others.
Lesson: Faith in God, Mankind and ourselves. Trust in victory over evil, the advancement of humanity and the hereafter. Charity and Tolerance.
19 ° Scots Master Grand Pontiff – Each person learns from the past and how it affects the present. The law of Correspondences or Cause and Effect.
Lesson: To Master Right Thinking and Use of the Mind
20 ° Sovereign Prince of Masons or Master ad Vitam - helps one to comprehend Deity, forces of nature, good and evil.
Lesson: The ability to see opportunity and good in all things.
21 ° Prussian Knight or Patriarch Noachite – Negative energy and thinking, arrogance, defamation and cowardice are non-constructive attributes of a Master.
Lesson: Humility is the greatest power and it is one of the secrets to faith and peace of mind.
22 ° Knight of the Royal Ax or Prince of Libanus – This Degree is about ethics and character building. Becoming a better person by making the most of yourself for the benefit of all.
Lesson: Right Livelihood can be the highest service and a labor of love.
23 ° Knight of The Sun, The Prince Adept, The key to Masonry - God manifests itself in our love for truth, justice and nobility of soul.
Lesson: Realizing we are each unique but part of the whole.
24 ° Knight of Black Eagle and Grand Inspector – Holy Knight -   To better comprehend Truth.
Lesson: The lesson of this degree is to be true to ourselves, to stand for what is right and to be just in our lives today with a belief in God. To have the right view.
25 ° **Prince of the Royal Secret** – Looking for the good and best in all. Awaken to a world view of opportunity and creativity and power.
Lesson: Arm yourself with Faith and Knowingness. Self Understanding and Reflection.. Transcending Self and Holding the Power to cultivate Love.

The Loge de Parfaits in New Orleans in 1764 had initiated the first use of the above degrees in North America which was a colony of France, then the land was ceded to Spain, and then and the land was later ceded and sold to the USA. The above Haut or High Initiatory degrees are Rosicrucian, Masonic, Hermetic, Oriental, and Christian in their philosophical nature. This first Continental American "Rite of Perfection" Loge was "In Essence", the original American "Societe des Illumines" or Illuminati of America. This Lodge and These degrees Existed in Sovereign Form for the first time in History.

NOTE: Important essays that address many of these degrees are explained in the rest of this book. These above 25 degrees are reconstructions based on research of New Orleans Masonic and Mystical Documents and the European/Scandinavian references to the original 25 Franken/Morin Degree System. The Below Celtic Grades are included as a system of virtuous and localized secret degrees that impacted the Loge de Parfait in New Orleans.

9 Secret Principles and Grades and Degrees of the Celtic Rose Croix Master

The **Noble Grades or Virtues** are the spiritual and ethical code gleaned from various sources including the Poetic Edda [iv] (particularly the Hávamál), the Nordic Sagas, & Celtic Warrior Code along with Hermetic Roman and Greek Spiritual Teachings. These degrees and virtues are included because of the huge immigration into New Orleans in the 1700's included the Celtic and Central European Peoples. These are in theory "Pre-Christian" codes that existed before and during the Roman occupation of Europe. These are the values and character building concepts that were taught before Cesar and were later incorporated into the great religions.

These lessons are very important as part of the influence upon European and American Mystery Teachings.

1. **Grade #1 – Apprentice - The Lesson for this degree is: Strength is better than weakness.** Strength is something earned. Many Times strength emerges from humility. It takes willingness and effort to obtain strength. When we intentionally grow our strength or latent powers, we are able to meet opportunities or challenges with preparedness. Weakness can be in the form of mental, physical, or spiritual weakness. Upright living and balance can prevent most instances of weakness.

2. **Grade #2 – Illustrious Warrior - The Lesson for this degree is: Perseverance and Courage** is better than cowardice. Examples of courage are acting with boldness to help others or even maintain your responsibilities. In today's world, perseverance implies action. Taking action and not procrastinating. Without action, an idea can not even begin any movement or obtain energy that it needs to manifest.

3. **Grade #3 – Master of the Legion - The Lesson for this degree is: Discipline and Joy** are better than guilt. Sooner or later, we must learn when to work and when to enjoy life in its purest form.

4. **Grade #4 – Noble Chief of the Lodge - The Lesson for this degree is: Honor** which is better than dishonor. What is Honorable? Being honorable involves your thought, word and deed. A man of faith, service and charity and whose self control transcends all drama and hostility.

5. **Grade #5 – Lord of the Order - The Lesson for this degree is: Self Reliance & Freedom** is better than slavery. As they used to say, the "industrial-revolution worker system" was "Slavery by Debt." Thus, we must learn to break free of over-dependence or being tied down to anything that can cause self & family injury over the long-term. We must make the best of ourselves from a standpoint of mind, education, health, body, spirit, harmony and so forth, to allow ourselves to become free to express ourselves naturally and effectively. It is better, therefore, not to deny others their natural hunger to learn, grow, earn, succeed, and work.

6. **Grade #6 – Prince and Knight of the Rose Croix- The Lesson for this degree is: Hospitality and Kinship** is better than alienation. Hospitality was a word that implied helping our brothers and sisters. The word Charity is most often used in our busy lives today. What is the key to the concept of hospitality? Is it "loving thy neighbor" as ourselves? By helping those who want to help themselves and being of service to those who can't, we open the door for the universe to shower us with opportunity and gifts.

7. **Grade #7 - Master Architect - The Lesson for this degree is: Truth and Realism** is better than dogmatism. What is the truth? Do we know the facts? Should we try to learn more? Do we have time to investigate? Do we need to take action? Is the meaning that we have attached to the truth destructive or constructive or simply based on ego or delusional mind?

8. **Grade #8 - Adept of the Rosy Cross - The Lesson for this degree is: Industriousness and Vigor** are better than lifelessness. As we know, doing 2 or 3 things per day effectively can add to a mountain of advantages during a lifetime. If we can help ourselves and help others, the entire family and community benefits and excels.

9. **Grade #9 Magus of the Rose Croix – The Lesson for this degree is: Fidelity** is better than universalism. Being true to yourself and following your dreams leads to your happiness and everyone else's happiness also. We are all unique and qualified to be our best in whatever endeavor we can achieve. We must make decisions, we must take positions, and we must take action. Sometimes we must chose sides. With that having been said, we must be strategic with our decisions while also trying to intelligently foresee the consequences of each of our individual decisions. Fidelity flows to our family and duty and obligation to the clan or family group. Members of the family who are open to suggestion and seek to better themselves to become self-reliant should be assisted.

*The above styled higher degrees were common in Nouvelle-Orléans over the last 250 years. Many of the Orleans degrees are extinct as of today and have not been conferred for many years. As a point of reference, The earliest recorded Central European German immigrants to Louisiana arrived in 1722 and were quite fond of clubs and societies. These included the popular United Ancient Order of the Druids. The first grove of Druids in the area, the Magnolia Hain (Magnolia Grove) was founded in 1836. Present-day visitors to the Odd Fellows Cemetery at the intersection of Canal Street and Metairie Road can see the tombs of the Germania Lodge Number 29 and of the Teutonia Lodge Number 10 with its inscription, "Freundschaft, Liebe, und Wahrheit" ("Friendship, Love, and Truth").

Part II. The Teachings, Essays, Metaphysics and Secrets.

Laws of Attraction & Mental Attitude

We must assert that all thinking, observant people have noticed the operation of the ancient mental Law of Attraction, whereby "Like Attracts Like." A man's Mental Attitude acts as a *magnet,* attracting to him the things, objects, circumstances, environments, and people in harmony with that Mental Attitude. *Fix your mind firmly upon anything, good or bad, in the world, and you attract it to you or are attracted to it in obedience to the LAW. You attract to you the character, ideals, people, and things you expect, think about and hold in your Mental Attitude with strong desire.*

Desire is the motivating force that moves the Will into action, and which cause the varied activity of life, men and things. Desire-Force is a real power in life, and influences not only tracts, influences and compels other persons and things to swing in toward the center of the Desire sending forth the currents. In the Secret of Success, Desire plays a prominent part. Without a Burning Desire for Success, there is no Direction. The Law of Attraction is set into motion by Desire. What is the pattern upon which the Law of Attraction builds under the force of Desire? The Mental Image, of course. The method of the action of Mental Attitude towards Spiritual Abundance may be called the working of the Law of Attraction. Now without attempting to advance any wild theories, I must assert that all thinking, observing men have noticed the operation of a mental Law of Attraction, whereby "like attracts like." A person's Mental Attitude acts as a magnet, attracting the things, objects, circumstances, environments, and people in harmony with that Mental Status and Attitude. Fix your mind firmly upon anything, good or bad, in the world, and you attract it to you or are attracted to it in obedience to the LAW. You attract to you the things you expect, what you think about, what you are willing to have, and to whatever you direct and focus in your Mental Energy.

The person who thinks, talks, and expects health and prosperity attracts these good things into their life. Sweep out from the chambers of your mind any negative thoughts and FILL up the mind with the strong, constructive, positive, invigorating, helpful, forceful, compelling thoughts and ideas such as: Success, Confidence, Health, Peace of Mind, and The Expectation of that which you desire. And, just as the steel fillings fly to the attraction of the magnet, so will that which you need fly to you in response to this great natural principle of mental action - the Law of Attraction. Begin this very moment and build up a new a new character of thinking and ideal - that of Peace, Health, Financial Independence and Abundance. See it mentally - expect it - demand it! This is the way to create it in your Enhanced Spiritual & Mental Attitude of Prosperity. The laws of life await your unlocking of the treasure chest of prosperity and abundant life.[v] Change your thoughts, and you will change your Destiny. [vi]

Karma and Correspondences

We see how very important is the Thoughts, Attention and The Feelings we have concerning anything, for upon the quality of our thought and concentration hinges the results and destiny that we manifest for ourselves. As a mental exercise, REMEMBER: All is right with the world. It is perfect and advancing to completion. I will contemplate the facts of social, political, and industrial life only from this high viewpoint. Behold, it is all very good. I will see all human beings, all my acquaintances, friends, neighbors, and the members of my own household in the same way. They are all good. Nothing is wrong with the universe; nothing can be wrong but my own personal attitude, and henceforth I keep that right. My whole trust is in God. The only service you can render God is to give expression to what he is trying to give the world, through you. The highest service you can render God is to make the very most of yourself in order that God may live in you to the utmost of your possibilities. In this way of mental and spiritual health, you can best serve those you love.

Overall, it has been said that repeated thoughts become tendencies or habits, willingness can become action, and repeated experiences lead to wisdom. Our thoughts, actions, inactions and omissions are what creates our character. If we desire good Karma Energy, we must be willing to put out good thoughts, praise others, become thankful, see things in a opportunistic light, have faith in the regeneration of mind and body and take right actions. Our every action and thought of goodness is very powerful. Acts of kindness, service to others, and self development are all extremely powerful energies. Thoughts of negative things are weak thoughts which are 100 times less powerful that acts of creation and constructiveness. If we maintain a harmonious relationship with the

Supreme Intelligence while keeping a peaceful relationship with our externals, life will, of course, be much easier. Further, when we are avoiding wasteful thinking and actions, our spiritual energies maintain a laser focus and power. As with Physics, it is possible to neutralize a sound wave by setting up another sound wave of the same pattern which comes from the opposite pole. Therefore, it is possible to conjure and visualize ideas, thoughts and images that can completely neutralize old attitudes. By changing our outlook, you can change your future. Every cause has its effect and every action has its results, but it is desire that is the link that connects the two.

Atonement and Purity of Mind

The Rosicrucian Mystery teaching gives a scientific method whereby an aspirant may purge himself continually of negative Karmic Energy. Each night after retiring the pupil reviews his life during the past day in reverse order. He starts to visualize as clearly as possible the scene which took place just before retiring. He then endeavors to impartially view his actions in that scene examining them to see whether he did right or wrong. If there is something that needs improvement, realize what you have done as vividly as possible, and try to feel exactly as that one felt whom was wronged and at the very earliest opportunity attempt to make amends or mental atonement for the hasty expression. Then, call up the next scene one by one, and endeavor to overcome any counterproductive habits.[vii]

Other Steps to the Mastery of Attunement

1. Humility, remaining teachable, and being right sized with regard to ego.
2. Developing character through change and growth
3. Honesty and Integrity (doing what you say and being honest with yourself)
4. Purity of Thought Heart and Intentions i.e. right thinking toward sobriety
5. Selflessness through giving without expectation of return through service and non-hoarding of yourself
6. Development of purpose, making healthy decisions, and being definite toward self improvement
7. Gratitude - Being thankful for the gifts you have received, praising others, blessing your home, family, and world
8. Willing to engage self analysis & evaluation for growth
9. Attunement toward harmony with others through amends, restitution, mental catharsis, character development, and right action.
10. Use of visualization, prayer, or meditation to enable a mental vision of a fuller life and connection to the universe.
11. Willingness to be open minded toward accepting a state of well being and peace of mind.
12. Allowing harmony in your life and a sincere belief that life is abundant.

The Power of Prayer and Meditation

Prayer and meditation must be for the good of all concerned. To effectively pray, you must petition the universal intelligence. You must create a harmonious relationship with the supreme so that you can release your creative thoughts and prayers to the universe. You must form a clear and definite mental picture of what you want. You cannot transmit an idea unless you have it yourself. You must have it before you can give it, and many people fail to impress universal intelligence because they have themselves only a vague and misty concept of the things they want to do, to have, or to become. It is not enough that you should have a general desire for wealth "with which to do good." Everybody has that desire.

It is not enough that you should have a wish to travel, see things, live more, etc. Everybody has those desires also. If you were going to send a wireless message to a friend, you would not send the letters of the alphabet in their order and let him construct the message for himself, nor would you take words at random from the dictionary. You would send a coherent sentence, one, which had real specific meaning. When you try to impress your wants upon the thinking substance, remember that it must be done with a coherent statement. You must know what you want and be specific and definite. You can never get rich or start the creative power into action by sending out unformed longings and vague desires. Go over your desires and objectives clearly and specifically. See just what you want and get a clear mental picture of it as you wish it to look when you get it. That clear mental picture you must have continually in mind.

As the sailor has in mind the port toward which he is sailing the ship, you must keep your face toward it all the time. You must no more lose sight of it than the helmsman loses sight of the compass. It is not necessary to take exercises in concentration, nor to set apart special times for prayer and affirmation, nor to "go into the silence," nor to do occult stunts of any kind. Some of these things are well enough, but all you need is to know what you want and to want it badly enough so that it will stay in your thoughts. Spend as much of your leisure time as you can in contemplating your picture. But no one needs to take exercises to concentrate his mind on a thing, which he really wants. It is the things you do not really care about which require effort to fix your attention upon them. And unless you really want to get rich, so that the desire is strong enough to hold your thoughts directed to the purpose as the magnetic pole holds the needle of the compass, it will hardly be worthwhile for you to try to carry out the instructions given in this book.

The methods set forth here are for people whose desire for growth and expansion is strong enough to overcome mental laziness and the love of ease, and to make them work. The more clear and definite you make your picture then, and the more you dwell upon it, bringing out all its delightful details, the stronger your desire will be. And the stronger your desire, the easier it will be to hold your mind fixed upon the picture of what you want. Something more is necessary, however, than merely to see the picture clearly. If that is all you do, you are only a dreamer, and will have little or no power for accomplishment.

Behind your clear vision must be the purpose to realize it, to bring it out in tangible expression. And behind this purpose must be an invincible and unwavering FAITH that the thing is already yours that it is "at hand" and you have only to take possession of it. Live in the new way or home, mentally, until it takes form around you physically. In the mental realm, enter at once into full enjoyment of the things you want.

"Whatsoever things ye ask for when ye pray, believe that ye receive them, and ye shall have them," said Jesus. See the things you want as if they were actually around you all the time. See yourself as owning and using them. Make use of them in imagination just as you will use them when they are your tangible possessions. Dwell upon your mental picture until it is clear and distinct, and then take the mental attitude of ownership toward everything in that picture. Take possession of it, in mind, in the full faith that it is actually yours. Hold to this mental ownership. Do not waiver for an instant in the faith that it is real. And remember what was said in a proceeding chapter about gratitude: Be as thankful for it all the time as you expect to be when it has taken form. The person who can sincerely thank God for the things that as yet he owns only in imagination has real faith. He will get rich. He will cause the creation of whatever he wants.

You do not need to pray repeatedly for things you want. It is not necessary to tell God about it every day. Your part is to intelligently formulate your desire for the things which make for a larger life and to get these desire arranged into a coherent whole, and then to impress this whole desire upon the formless substance, which has the power and the will to bring you what you want. You do not make this impression by repeating strings of words; you make it by holding the vision with unshakable PURPOSE to attain it and with steadfast FAITH that you do attain it.

The answer to prayer is not according to your faith while you are talking, but according to your faith while you are working. Keep yourself focused and thinking in the certain way with of words; you make it by holding the vision with unshakable PURPOSE to attain it and with steadfast FAITH that you do attain it. The answer to prayer is not according to your faith while you are talking, but according to your faith while you are working. You cannot impress the mind of God by having a special Sabbath day set apart to tell him what you want, and then forgetting him during the rest of the week. You cannot impress him by having special hours to go into your closet and pray, if you then dismiss the matter from your mind until the hour of prayer comes again. Oral prayer is well enough, and has its effect, especially upon yourself, in clarifying your vision and strengthening your faith, but it is not your oral petitions that get you what you want. In order to get rich you do not need a "sweet hour of prayer;" you need to "pray without ceasing." And by prayer I mean holding steadily to your vision, with the purpose to cause its creation into solid form, and the faith that you are doing so. "Believe that ye receive them."

Once you have clearly formed your vision, the whole matter turns on receiving. When you have formed it, it is well to make an oral statement, addressing the supreme in gratitude. Then, from that moment on you must, in mind, receive what you ask for. Live in the new house, wear the fine clothes, ride in the automobile, go on the journey, and confidently plan for greater journeys. Think and speak of all the things or ideals or health that you have asked for in terms of actual present ownership. Imagine an environment and a condition exactly as you want them, and live all the time in that mental environment and financial condition until they take physical shape. Mind, however, that you do not do this as a mere dreamer and castle builder. Hold to the FAITH that the imaginary is being realized and to your PURPOSE to realize it. Remember that it is faith and purpose in the use of the imagination that make the difference between the scientist and the dreamer. [viii]

7 Cosmic Principles -   Rosicrucian & Hermetic – The Kyballion Laws

The Kybalion was first published in December of 1908 by The Three Initiates who was probably Dr. William Walker Atkinson and his associates. The book addressed Hermeticism and the Ancient Mysteries of the Greek and Egyptian Empires. The Kybalion states that the book was published by Yogi Publication Society. Some calculate that the Kybalion is an work of an older Greek manuscript called the Kabalyon from several thousand years ago. These 7 laws are said to be the essence of the teachings of Hermes Trismegistus and his Alchemy. These laws are also published in almost identical fashion in various Rosicrucian Manifestos.

The Kybalion speaks of 2 major metaphysical issues: 1) The ALL in All and 2) Correspondences and Cause and Effect.

The "All in All" can be related to the reasoning that we are part of ALL and the Supreme. We are however, connected to ALL and we contain a part of it. It is self-evident therefore, that we are connected to all being, life, and universal substance. The ALL, moreover, contains all of what we are. With this in mind, it parallels many of the Ancient Eastern Mystics such as: Christians such as Meister Eckhart, Buddha, Vedic Teachings, Socrates, Swedenborg, and more. Additionally, if we are part and connected to all, we can communicate to all via the Hermetic Teachings of Mentalism, Vibration, Cause and Effect and our Mind Thoughts and Actions.

With the law of cause and effect, we know that even Plato and Aristotle realized that every effect has a cause. There is a chain of events and mind stuff that leads to every outcome. Although we may not cause every specific outcome, we play a part in each chain of causation.

With vibrations, many teachers are explaining to students how to affect their personal vibratory and rhythmic rates of thinking, moods, and even prayer and meditation. With concentration, focus, and mental imaging, we can affect our future and the energy that precedes us.

Notes on The Seven Hermetic Principles

I. THE PRINCIPLE OF MENTALISM
We are Spirit and are part of ALL, our minds must work in tune with the infinite. Thus, we have a duty to mentally work in harmony with the spirit within and without. The closer we bring ourselves to the source of all, the closer it will draw to us. There is a connecting link between us and the ALL that we can clog up or block with the emotions of: pride, fear, or anger etc. Thus, the goal is that mind and spirit within can work in accordance with the spirit throughout and surrounding us. We must meet the All half-way with our thought and action

II. THE PRINCIPLE OF CORRESPONDENCE.

"As above, so below; as below, so above."—The Kybalion – With this statement we determine that our present and past mind function and focus corresponds with our reality. We can will our minds to focus or concentrate in any direction with which corresponding energy will meet us in the future. The Mind is the creator of the reality that we have and will have. Various influences may affect the path, but we can be in continuous contact with the universal forces which alters the journey. Realizing that the spirit energy of ALL is contained within is the breakthrough, but having a harmonious relationship with the spirit energy within and without is the key to initial & long-term prosperity.

III. THE PRINCIPLE OF VIBRATION.

Your vibration can be at many levels. To say the least, you can enhance your mental vibration through various actions. Higher levels of mental and spiritual vibrations include: Love, Gratitude, Praise, Faith, Feel good emotions and more. Many practitioners work on a daily basis to enhance and bring their mental and spiritual vibration to a higher level. Practitioners do this so that they may lead a more harmonious life, but also to attract people, events and things of the same or higher vibration. The end result of healthy vibrations is the attraction of more constructive events, outcomes, and possibilities.

IV. THE PRINCIPLE OF POLARITY.

All things and issues have 2 sides. As stated by the Hermetics, cold and heat are degrees or fluctuations of the same thing such as climate. Other examples include love and dislike or truth or half-truth. There are 2 sides to everything, thus looking beyond what is apparent and searching deeper for the truth is important. Why is this important? The understanding of the poles and truths allows us to flow with the world instead of fighting events. This is because we are able to respond in a spiritual manner until we understand the event better. As an example, something may happen that is NOT a result that we wanted. However, after continuing our efforts and moving forward with action, we may find that something better is coming to us in due time. When we are in tune with the spirit and energy of all, we are able to best respond to happenings in a spiritual way. Without reacting, we maintain our composure, focus on today and continue to move forward without engaging a senseless battle. From this flow and patience, we are able to bring even higher prosperity, greater success, and peace of mind to ourselves.

V. THE PRINCIPLE OF RHYTHM.

Life and events can swing like a pendulum. A practitioner can learn to control their mind and spirit energy to keep harmony through life's ebb and flow of events, personalities and thought. As an example, you can neutralize your destructive thoughts with thoughts of: Blessing, Praise, Love, Gratitude, Acceptance, and Faith. Even in instances of envy or doubt, we must continue to praise our homes, spouses, children, & other people of success and wealth, and friends. When we bless and mentally praise others, we dissipate any fears and jealous thoughts and therefore attract wealth, health and peace of mind in our own field of energy.

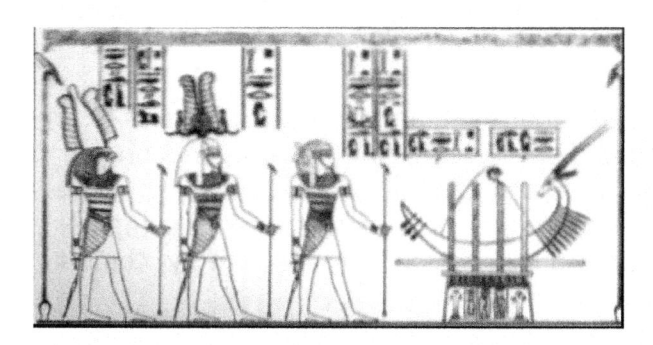

VI.   THE PRINCIPLE OF CAUSE AND EFFECT.

For every thought, action or inaction, there is a corresponding thought and event. Your heartfelt emotions when mixed with constructive thought and action carry more force than the average thought and action. Building a foundation is vital to this step. At first, we must change our mentality from one of lack to a consciousness and mind of possibility. Our minds and hearts evolve and begin to believe in opportunity and abundance. Instead of thinking why, we transcend to a spiritual position of why not. At this juncture, we begin to take action in accordance with our dreams. Each mental and physical action we take on a daily basis adds to the momentum of our spiritual force. Our spiritual force in conjunction with our harmonious and constructive thinking begins to manifest higher realities in our days to come.

VII. THE PRINCIPLE OF GENDER.

Each person or event may have a gender-like energy built into it. Learning what energy is at the heart of each issue or situation is very helpful. The practitioner may be able to better work with events and people if they understand the underlying energy of it. Understanding the feelings, emotions, logic, and purpose of each person, place or event can allow us to work better with it or even allow us to avoid it if necessary. The teachings herein include statements about the Conscious and Subconscious Mind and the I and Me. Thus, there is a WITHIN component to this principle. Each person must understand that their mind is like a computer but you are the operator. You must realize that what you engrave upon your hard drive can affect your Operating System and your Memory and function.

Further, if you clear your mind and spirit via exercises of prayer, affirmations, good diet, exercise, and self examination you can also improve your spiritual and mental function much like a virus software or a charged battery can clear out the junk from your computer and improve performance. Once again, in your mind is both the computer and the [I AM] operator of the computer.

Both have a voice. Knowing which one is speaking to you takes some effort and concentration. As a note, many people have been pre-programmed from family, friends, and exposure. This programming may have your hard drive overloaded with no room for advancement. Knowing how to clear out the hard drive and defragment the drive is important. Your intuition will speak to you if you need to work on this type of catharsis.

The Synthesis of the Ancient Greco-Egyptian Hermetic Principles

It can be said that a master of the 7 principles has become spiritually awakened from the state of illusions. When effectively working the

Hermetic steps herein, the practitioner's awareness can be opened where they are in tune with the infinite. When a person opens their eyes, mind, senses, and heart to opportunity, life, bliss, creation and love, the world can blossom before their eyes on each waking day. Instead of waking up believing in doom and gloom, the practitioner is waking up expecting the cooperation of the world, universe and spirit. While recognizing the source of the power, the adherent also manages his or her thoughts, mental vibration, and spirit rhythm so as to radiate only the best energy to the source and to others operating on this physical plane.

Remember, your force and energy is yours to protect and strengthen. Don't let others tap into it and try and drain you. Using these principles, you see that your energy can be augmented, drained or tainted. Other people who do not understand your force, may carry negative energy or particles that can enter your wave or field. You understand that your mental and spiritual focus on strength, happiness, success, prosperity, health, faith and confidence will keep your field strong. However, other tainted people may carry particles that are somewhat contagious. Examples are: Complainers, Fear Mongers, and Pessimists. The only way for you to deal with these people is to convey your optimism, avoid them, or neutralize them with thoughts and feelings of love, compassion, and peace. Never bother fighting them and simply allow them to be. All is right with your world, and you need not try to change them in any drastic manner. Your action, faith, character, and prosperity will eventually gain their attention and respect. If not, it is wise to avoid their manipulation. As with probabilities, each person may have many destinations but engages only one plane of the journey at a time. Thus, simple actions and causes can put you on another fork of possibility in the chain of causation. Knowing how to take action or maneuver the energies and opportunities in the external world will allow you to make positive and constructive choices on your path. As you know, faith is an expectation of something better and good on a daily basis. Faith involves confidence and resolve over your constructive beliefs. As an example, scientists say that the earth has magma at its core, but nobody has ever been to earth's center. We just take it as fact.

The Hermetic Master knows that pure spirit is at the core of the Source of All there is based on their experience and working with the art of cooperating with the Source of ALL. In the same way, every person of intellect knows that bad germs and parasites can destroy an unhealthy host. Scientists also know that there are healthy forms of inner agents such as white blood cells or other natural immunities. Therefore, the master understands how to strengthen inner supply, attract healthy agents, and also to become immune to unhealthy forces by neutralizing them. By doing this, you can enter the 4th dimension of peace, love, confidence, and prosperity. Understanding the energy of other beings or forces, allows the master to interrelate on this earthly plane in the most effective manner without harm. The person who best employs these secrets will reach heightened awareness and keep a calm focus on their purpose using their powers effectively each day. The end result is prosperity, health, harmony, growth, and peace. [ix]

Hermes Trismegistus, floor mosaic in the Cathedral of Siena

Emerald Tablets

The *Emerald Tablet*, also known as *Smaragdine Table*, *Tabula Smaragdina*, or *The Secret of Hermes*, are ancient writings that may reveal the secrets of the fundamental substance and the alchemical attributes thereof. It claims to be the work of Hermes Trismegistus ("Hermes the Thrice-Great"),

The most famous Egyptian guru.[x] Using these tablets is what has allowed philosophers to utilize the 7 Hermetic Principles.

1. True, without error, certain and most true 2. That which is below is as that which is above, and that which is above is as that which is below, to perform the miracles of the one thing. 3. And as all things were from [the] one, by [means of] the meditation of [the] one, thus all things of the daughter from [the] one, by [means of] adaptation. 4. Its father is the sun, its mother[,]the moon, the wind carried it in its belly, its nurse is the earth. 5. The father of all the initiates of the whole world is here. 6. Its power is integrating if it be turned into earth. 7. Separate the earth from the fire, the fine from the dense, delicately, by [means of/to] the great [together] with capacity. 8. It ascends by [means of] earth into heaven and again it descends into the earth, and retakes the power of the superior[s] and of the inferior[s]. 9. Thus[,] you have the glory of the whole world. 10. Therefore[,] may it drive-out by [means of] you of all the obscurity. 11. This is the whole of the strength of the strong force, because it overcomes all fine things, and penetrates all the complete. 12. Thus[,] the world has been created. 13. Hence they were wonderful adaptations, of which this is the manner. 14. Therefore[,] I am Hermes the Thrice Great, having the three parts of the philosophy of the whole world. 15. What I have said concerning the operation of the Sun has been completed.

Desire and Purpose

Desire is the motivating force that runs the world; as little as we care to admit it in many cases. Look around you and see the effects of Desire in every human act, good or bad. As a writer has said:"Every deed that we do, good or bad, is prompted by Desire. Desire is the motivating power behind all actions – it is a natural law of life. Everything from the atom to the monad; from the monad to the insect; from the insect to man; from man to Nature, acts and does things by reason of the power and force of Desire, the Animating Motive. " All the above at the first glance would seem to make of man a mere machine, subject to the power of any stray desire that might happen to come into his mind. But this is far from being so. Man acts not upon EVERY desire, but upon the STRONGEST Desire, or the Average of his Strongest Desires. This FOCUS of your Desires is that which constitutes your Nature or Character. And here is where the Mastery of the "I" comes in. Man need not be a slave or creature of his Desires if he will assert his Mastery. He may control, regulate, govern and guide his Desires in any directions that he pleases. Nay, more, he may even CREATE DESIRES by an action of his Will, as we shall see presently. By a knowledge of psychological laws he may neutralize unfavorable Desires, and grow and develop – yes, practically Create New Desires in their place – all by the power of his Will, aided by the light of his Reason and Judgment. Man is the Master of his Mind.

"Yes," but some close reasoning critic may object; "yes, that is true enough, but even in that case is not Desire the ruling motive – must not one Desire create these new Desires before he can do so – is not Desire always precedent to action? "Very close reasoning this, good friends, but all advanced metaphysicians know that there is a point in which the Principle of Desire shades and merges into companion Principle, Will, and that a practitioner may imagine a mental state in which one may be almost said to manifest a WILL to Will, rather than to merely Desire to Will. This state must be experienced before it can be understood – words cannot express it.

Dismiss the old negative ideas of mind and create new ones in their places. And here is how it may be done: In the first place, one must think carefully over the tasks that he wishes to accomplish, then, using his judgment carefully, judicially and impartially – impersonally so far as is possible – he must take mental stock of himself and see in what points he is deficient, so far as the successful accomplishment of the task is concerned. Then let him analyze the task before him, in detail, separating the matter into as many clear defined divisions as possible, so that he may be able to see the Thing as It Is, in detail as well as in its entirety. Then let him take a similar inventory of the things, which seem necessary of the accomplishment of the task – not the details that will arise only as the work progresses, day by day – but the general things, which must be done in order that the task is brought to a successful conclusion. Then having taken stock of the task, the nature of the undertaking, and one's own qualifications and shortcomings – then Begin to Create Desire, according to the following plan: The first step in the Creation of Desire is that of the forming of a clear, vital Mental Image of the qualities, things and details of the undertaking, as well as of the Completed Whole. By a Mental Image we mean a clear-cut, distinct mental picture in the Imagination. Imagination is a real thing – it is a faculty of the mind by which it creates a matrix, mold, or pattern of things, which the trained Will and Desire afterward, materializes into objective reality. There has been nothing created by the hands and mind of man which did not have its first origin in the Imagination of some one. Imagination is the first step in Creation – whether of worlds or trifles. The mental pattern must always precede the material form. And so it is in the Creation of Desire. Before you can Create a Desire you must have a clear Mental Image of what you need to Desire. Practice makes perfect. Each time you try to form the Mental Image it will appear a little clearer and more distinct, and the details will come into a little more prominence. Do not tire yourself at first, but lay aside the task until later in the day, or tomorrow. But practice and persevere and you need, just as clearly as a memory picture of something you have already seen. We shall have more to say on this subject of Mental Imagery and Imagination in subsequent lessons. Then, after having acquired the clear Mental Image of the things you wish to Desire, and thus attain, cultivate the focusing of the Attention upon these things. The word attention is derived from the Latin word "Attendere," meaning "to stretch forth," the original idea being that in Attention the mind was "stretched forth," or "extended" toward the object of attention, and this is the correct idea for that is the way the mind operates in the matter. Keep the ideas before your attention as much as possible, so that the mind may take a firm grasp upon them, and make them a part of itself – by doing this you firmly impress the ideas upon the wax tablet of the mind. Thus having fixed the idea clearly in your mind, by means of the Imagination and Attention, until as we have said, it becomes a fixture there, begin to cultivate an ardent DESIRE, LONGING, CRAVING DEMAND for the materialization of the things. Demand that you grow the qualities necessary for the task – demand that your mental pictures materialize – Demand that the details be manifested as well as the Whole, making allowance for the "something better" which will surely arise to take the place of the original details, as you proceed – the Inner Consciousness will attend to these things for you. Then, proceed to hold your Desire in mind, firmly, confident, and earnestly. Be not half-hearted in your purpose and desires – claim and demand the WHOLE THING, and feel confident that it will work out into material objectivity and reality. Think of it, dream of it, and always LONG for it – you must learn to want it the worst way – learn to "want it hard enough. "You can attain and obtain many things by "wanting them hard enough" – the trouble is with most of us that we do not want things hard enough, and we mistake vague cravings for real wants or purposeful desires . Get to Desire and Earnestly Want the Essence of the Thing just as you demand and Desire your daily meals. That is what we mean by: "wanting it the worst way." People need food, water, sunshine, love and more. Your purpose and the will behind you true place is demanding expression inside of you. You spirit is seeking natural unfoldment.

Schools of philosophy, notably that founded by Schopenhauer, have also postulated the presence of a Universal Spirit (whose chief attribute is Desire-Will) from whom the universe of creatures has proceeded. This Universal Spirit is held to be filled with a longing, craving, seeking, striving desire to express itself in phenomenal existence. Schopenhauer calls it "The Will to Live." It is described as instinctive rather than intellectual, and as creating intellect with which to better serve its purposes of self-expression. Other philosophers have proceeded along the main lines of the concept of Schopenhauer, with various modifications. The same idea is expressed by some of the old Vedic, Taoist or Buddhistic philosophers, the very term Tao being used to express the essential nature of the Universal Spirit. But, it must be noted, in such philosophies, the Universal Spirit is considered rather as the Eternal Parent than as its First Manifestation. In the same way a certain school of thinkers postulate the existence of a "Living Nature," which expresses itself in innumerable living creatures and things--all Things in the universe being held to possess Life in some form and degree, as, indeed, the Rosicrucian creatures also hold.[xi] Accordingly, even in today's attitudes where science, philosophy, and religious metaphysics cross paths, most have acknowledge that purpose, natural expression, mission, and finding your true place are all major factors in self-expression and spirit-manifestation. Where a persons' true purpose is frustrated, reactions take place and most people are guided and again re-directed by their burning desires toward their highest ideal of creativeness and function. [xii]

Reincarnation, Reinvention, and Rebirth

Many people may debate about what happens to the soul after the death of the body. To put this discussion in a form that we all can understand, let us imagine that each day is a new birth and a new opportunity to live again and do the right thing while living under your highest ideals. Each night, our past-self can be allowed to die out and re-incarnate upon the following morning, and we can be born anew. Moreover, the purification, catharsis and sharpening of the mind is all part of the Rosicrucian transformation and transmutation methods. This discussion is particularly important with regard to karma and our actions each day. All men and women have the opportunity to: change, atone, grow, regenerate, become reborn and become awakened.

However, to be sure, some information on the subject in contained here. And so, Reincarnation is the great opportunity of man to start to build where construction has ceased. After a death of the ego-self which can happen at any moment, the soul can be malleable and in flux. Some call it openness or a "moment of clarity". We may be in this "rebirthing like" stage, much as the caterpillar in the cocoon. Our character and spirit can then act only through the law of desire, purpose, vibration & attraction. Dynamic changes and growth can occur rapidly from this state.

The soul must develop through the instrumentality of the mind. The Soul receives its impressions through the five senses of the body, and at birth, the period of development starts. Man is given that governor, that guide, that director, which has the power to use or discard all the forces of the universe in his ongoing. And that Director is the Mind. There can be no building without an ideal, a plan, and that plan, that ideal must be held by the mind. The mind thinks, and it sets to work all the great substances, the universe toward the accomplishment of its purpose, whether that purpose be toward construction or destruction.

Without the mind and spirit, the body would be as inert and inanimate as a piece of clay, without the power to create, or even move. The Mind is the governor, the constructor, the tool which shapes the destiny of man towards everlasting life, or toward the destruction of the body, in which latter event the soul must again go through the process of perfection in order to again have the opportunity which in its last incarnation rejected. And in this opportunity which is given man, he is placed, as is everything else in the universe, plant, planet, animal, God, under the law of cause and effect. God has endowed man with the greatest of all natural faculties, the Mind. As a man thinks, he creates, and he has the power and opportunity to create that which he wills. If he, through the knowledge of this law, and the love and ideal in his heart, should miss the mark of perfection, he, through the law of "change, catharsis, and rebirth", will be of such high vibration that he will be attracted in his next reinvention/incarnation to opportunities/parents who will give his soul every opportunity to express, in the highest environment, that which his soul craves. Do you remember how clearly the Bible states this, when Christ asks his disciples "Whom do men say that I am?"

And the answer is given that some said he was Elisha, and various of the other spiritually developed men who had lived before him. But when he asks his disciples, his faculties who he really believed himself to be, the answer, came, "Thou are the Christ, the son of the living God;" the goal, the ideal was thus established in his mind, and the building continued for its attainment.

Then what is the true lesson of Reincarnation? Is it necessary for us to die in order to be given another opportunity to build the ideal which should be in every heart ? Does God wish us to die? Can God die? Friends, true Reincarnation is the conscious, unceasing, unfaltering building into the mind and body, the ideal of the illumined Soul, and through the bringing forth of the illumined Soul, the inner spark of faith and enlightenment, the spiritual awakening, the becoming a child of God, the unchangeable, the imperishable energy of the supreme that which is through all time, and has all of the properties and powers of the universal spirit.

This awakening can occur by virtue of a shift of consciousness, a sacramental initiation, a molecular regeneration, a release of poison by private confession, a confirmation of your path, or a rebirth of the spirit.

Reincarnation to the student of the Soul, is the transmuting of the baser desires, the baser ideals, the baser metal, into that fine & pure ideal, and the conscious, loving, all-engrossing desire of the mind and heart to build that ideal here and now. Then there will be no more need to return and perfect that which before had been a failure; then will all the things be subject to the dominion of the soul which has attained spiritual peace and abundance. Then will the work have been finished, and sorrow and distress will have been banished from out of the life of such a one.[xiii]

The Leading Metaphysical Law

Whatever enters the consciousness of man will express itself in the personality of man. This is one of the most important of all the laws of life, and when its immense scope is fully comprehended thousands of perplexing questions will be answered. We shall then know why we are as we are and why all things about us are as they are; and we shall also know how all this can be changed. When we examine the principle upon which this law is based we find that our environments are the results of our actions, inactions and our omissions and are the results of our thoughts. Our physical and mental conditions are the results of our states of mind and our states of mind are the results of our ideas. Our thoughts are mental creations patterned after the impressions that exist in consciousness, and our ideas are the mental conceptions that come from our conscious understanding of life. Thus we realize that everything existing both in the mental field and in the personality, as well as in surrounding conditions, have their origin in that which becomes active in human consciousness.

We may define consciousness by stating that it is an attribute of the Ego through which the individual knows what is and what is taking place. Consciousness may usually be divided into three phases, the objective, the subjective and the absolute. Through absolute consciousness the Ego discerns its relationship with the universal—that phase of consciousness that is beyond the average mind and need not necessarily be considered in connection with this law. Through subjective consciousness the Ego knows what is taking place within itself, that is, within the vast field of individuality. And through objective consciousness the Ego knows what is taking place in its immediate external world. Objective consciousness employs the five external senses, while subjective consciousness employs all those finer perceptions which, when grouped together are sometimes spoken of as the sixth sense.

To employ this law properly nothing must be permitted to enter the subjective mind unless we wish to have it reproduced in ourselves. We should refuse therefore to take into consciousness that which we do not wish to see expressed through mind or body. We should allow ourselves to spiritually "LET GO" of the things that may continue to injure us. We should train consciousness to respond only to those external impressions that are desirable; and we should train our own imaging faculties to impress deeply and permanently in consciousness every good thing or desirable quality that we wish to see reproduced in ourselves and expressed through our personality.[xiv]

How the Mind Creates Your World and Character

Man gradually grows into the likeness of that which he thinks of the most.

Man is the reflection of all his thought; that is, his body, his character, his mind, his spiritual nature—all are fashioned according to his thought; This explains why refined thought refines every fiber of the body, improving the quality and perfecting the structure.

We should love the perfect, the divine and the spiritual in every soul in existence, and give the whole heart to the love of the sublime qualities of the Supreme. Thus we shall find that body, mind and soul will respond to the perfect thought that we thus form while living on the mental heights. Gradually we shall find all the elements of our nature changing for the better, becoming more and more like those sublime states of mind of which we are so vividly conscious. [xv]

The highest service you can render God is to give expression to what he is trying to give the world, through you. The only service you can render God is to make the very most of yourself in order that God may live in you to the utmost of your possibilities. As with a child on the piano for the first time attempting to express inner music, the music in a person's soul may not find expression through untrained hands. This is a good illustration of the way the Spirit of God is over, about, around, and in all of us, seeking to do great things with us, so soon as we will train our hands and feet, our minds, brains, and bodies to do his service.

WITHOUT faith it is impossible to have a harmonious and cooperative relationship with the God Force," and without faith it is impossible for you to become great and have a constructive world-view. The distinguishing characteristic of all really great men and women is an unwavering faith and knowingness of expectation. Faith-not a faith in one's self or in one's own powers but faith in principle; in the Something Great which upholds right, and which may be relied upon to give us the victory in due time. Without this faith, it is not possible for anyone to rise to real greatness. The man who has no faith in principle will always be a small man. Whether you have this faith or not depends upon your point of view. You must learn to see the world as being produced by growth change and expansion, as a something that is evolving and becoming, not as a finished work. Millions of years ago "The Creator" worked with very low and crude forms of life, low and crude, yet each perfect after its kind. Higher and more complex organisms, animal and vegetable, appeared through the successive ages; the earth passed through stage after stage in its unfolding, each stage perfect in itself, and to be succeeded by a higher one. What I wish you to note is that the so-called "lower organisms" are as perfect after their kind as the higher ones; but God's work was not finished. This is true of the world today. Physically, socially, and industrially, it is all good, and it is all perfect. It is not complete anywhere or in any part, but so far as the handiwork of God has gone, it is perfect.

THIS MUST BE YOUR POINT OF VIEW: THAT THE WORLD AND ALL IT CONTAINS IS PERFECT, THOUGH NOT COMPLETED. "All's right with the world." That is the great fact. There is nothing wrong with anything; there is nothing wrong with anybody. All the facts of life you must contemplate from this standpoint. There is nothing wrong with nature. Nature is a great advancing presence working beneficently for the happiness of all. All things in Nature are good; she has no evil. She is not completed; for creation is still unfinished, but she is going on to give to man even more bountifully than she has given to him in the past. Nature is a partial expression of God, and God is love. She is perfect but not complete.

So you see it makes a vast difference to you, this matter of the social viewpoint. "All's right with the world. Nothing can possibly be wrong but my personal attitude, and I will make that right. I will see the facts of nature and all the events, circumstances, and conditions of society, politics, government, and industry from the highest viewpoint. It is all perfect, though incomplete. It is all the handiwork of God; behold, it is all very good."

Make a thought-form of yourself, as you desire to be, and set your ideal as near to perfection as your imagination is capable of forming the conception. Let me illustrate: If a young law student wishes to become great, let him picture himself as a great lawyer, pleading his case with matchless eloquence and power before the judge and jury; as having an unlimited command of truth, of knowledge and of wisdom. Let him picture himself as the great attorney in every possible situation and contingency. While he is still only the student in all circumstances, let him never forget or fail to be the great lawyer in his thought-form of himself. As the thought-form grows more definite and habitual in his mind, the creative energies, both within and without, are set at work, and he begins to manifest the form from within and all the essentials without, which go into the picture, begin to be impelled toward him. He makes himself into the image and God works with him; nothing can prevent him from becoming what he wishes to be.

In the same general way the musical student pictures himself as performing perfect harmonies, and as delighting vast audiences; the actor forms the highest conception he is capable of in regard to his art, and applies this conception to himself. The farmer and the mechanic do exactly the same thing. Fix upon your ideal of what you wish to make of yourself; consider well and be sure that you make the right choice; that is, the one that will be the most satisfactory to you in a general way. Do not pay too much attention to the advice or suggestions of those around you: do not believe that any one can know, better than yourself, what is right for you. Listen to what others have to say, but always form your own conclusions. DO NOT LET OTHER PEOPLE DECIDE WHAT YOU ARE TO BE. BE WHAT

YOU FEEL THAT YOU WANT TO BE. Do not be misled by a false notion of obligation or duty. You can owe no possible obligation or duty to others that should prevent you from making the most of yourself. Be true to yourself, and you cannot then be false to any man. When you have fully decided what thing you want to be, form the highest conception of that thing that you are capable of imagining, and make that conception a thought-form. Hold that thought-form as a fact, as the real truth about yourself, and believe in it.

Close your ears to all adverse suggestions. Never mind if people call you a fool and a dreamer. Dream on. Remember great leaders and entrepreneurs that have come from nothing. Ideas are what is your power, and all you need is to continue to grow, be open minded, decide what you want to be and become bold as to the development of your character.

Affirmation: There is THAT in me of which I am made, which knows no imperfection, weakness, or sickness. The world is incomplete, but God in my own consciousness is both perfect and complete. Nothing can be wrong but my own personal attitude, and my own personal attitude can be wrong only when I disobey THAT which is within. I am a perfect manifestation of God so far as I have gone, and I will press on to be complete. I will trust and not be afraid." When you are able to say this understandingly you will have lost all fear and you will be far advanced upon the road to the development of a great and powerful personality. [xvi]

How Mental Pictures Become Realities

A person is a thinking centre and can originate thought. All the forms that a person fashions with his hands must first exist in his thought. He cannot shape a thing until he has thought that thing. Thought is the only power which can produce tangible results from the formless substance. The stuff from which all things are made is a substance that thinks, and a thought of form in this substance produces the form. Original substance moves according to its thoughts; every form and process you see in nature is the visible expression of a thought in original substance. As the formless stuff thinks of a form, it takes that form; as it thinks of a motion, it makes that motion. That is the way all things were created.

We live in a thought world, which is part of a thought universe. The thought of a moving universe extended throughout formless substance, and the thinking stuff — moving according to that thought — took the form of systems of planets, and maintains that form. Thinking substance takes the form of its thought, and moves according to the thought. Holding the idea of a circling system of suns and worlds, it takes the form of these bodies, and moves them as it thinks. Thinking the form of a slow-growing oak tree, it moves accordingly, and produces the tree, though centuries may be required to do the work. In creating, the formless seems to move according to the lines of motion it has established. In other words, the thought of an oak tree does not cause the instant formation of a full-grown tree, but it does start in motion the forces, which will produce the tree, along established lines of growth.

Every thought of form, held in thinking substance, causes the creation of the form, but always, or at least generally, along lines of growth and action already established. The thought of a house of a certain construction, if it were impressed upon formless substance, might not cause the instant formation of the house, but it would cause the turning of creative energies already working in trade and commerce into such channels as to result in the speedy building of the house. And if there were no existing channels through which the creative energy could work, then the house would be formed directly from primal substance, without waiting for the slow processes of the organic and inorganic world.

Substance is friendly to you, and is more anxious to give you what you want than you are to get it. To get rich, you need only to use your will power upon yourself. When you know what to think and do, then you must use your will to compel yourself to think and do the right things. That is the legitimate use of the will in getting what you want — to use it in holding yourself to the right course. Use your will to keep yourself thinking and acting in the certain way. Do not try to project your will, or your thoughts, or your mind out into space to "act" on things or people. Keep your mind at home. It can accomplish more there than elsewhere. Use your mind to form a mental image of what you want and to hold that vision with faith and purpose. And use your will to keep your mind working in the right way. The more steady and continuous your faith and purpose, the more rapidly you will get rich because you will make only POSITIVE impressions upon substance, and you will not neutralize or offset them by negative impressions.

The picture of your desires, held with faith and purpose, is taken up by the formless, and permeates it to great distances — throughout the universe, for all we know. As this impression spreads, all things are set moving toward its realization. Every living thing, every inanimate thing, and the things yet uncreated are stirred toward bringing into being that which you want. All force begins to be exerted in that direction. All things begin to move toward you. The minds of people everywhere are influenced toward doing the things necessary to the fulfilling of your desires, and they work for you, unconsciously. [xvii]

The mind is very large. It is therefore possible to form mental pictures of as many ideals as we like, but at first it is best to choose only a few. Begin by picturing a perfect body, an able mind a strong character and a beautiful soul; after that an ideal interior life and an ideal external environment. Thus you have the foundation of a great life, a rich life and a wonderful life. Keep these pictures constantly before your mind—in fact, train yourself to actually live joyfully and knowingly in conjunction with your mental pictures. And you will find all things in your life changing daily to become more and more like those ideal images in your mental possession. In the course of time you will realize in actual life the unique likeness of those pictures; that is, what you have constantly seen upon your mental picture screen is what you will realize in actual life. Then you can form new and more beautiful images to be realized in like manner as you build for a still greater future. [xviii]

There is a thinking stuff from which all things are made, and which, in its original state, permeates, penetrates, and fills the interspaces of the universe. A thought in this substance produces the thing that is imaged by the thought. A person can form things in his thought, and, by impressing his thought upon formless substance, can cause the thing he thinks about to be created. In order to do this, a person must pass from the competitive to the creative mind; he must form a clear mental picture of the things he wants, and hold this picture in his thoughts with the fixed PURPOSE to get what he wants, and the unwavering FAITH that he does get what he wants, closing his mind against all that may tend to shake his purpose, dim his vision, or quench his faith. And in addition to all this, we shall now see that he must live and act in a certain way.[xix] As you go forward in an effective way, opportunities will come to you in increasing number, and you will need to be very steady in your faith and purpose, and to keep in close touch with the supreme mind by reverent gratitude.

Do all that you can do in a perfect manner every day, but do it without haste, worry, or fear. Go as fast as you can, but never hurry. Remember that in the moment you begin to hurry you cease to be a creator and become a competitor. You drop back upon the old plane again. Whenever you find yourself hurrying, call a halt. Fix your attention on the mental image of the thing you want and begin to give thanks that you are getting it. The exercise of GRATITUDE will never fail to strengthen your faith and renew your purpose.

门茨

The Seventh Aphorism of Rosicrucianism

THE SEVENFOLD SOUL OF MAN
In the Secret Doctrine of the Rosicrucians, we find the following Seventh Aphorism:

The Soul of Man is Sevenfold, yet but One in essence; Man's Spiritual Unfoldment has as its end the Discovery of Himself beneath the Sevenfold Veil. In this Seventh Aphorism of Creation, the Rosicrucian is directed to apply his attention to the concept of the Sevenfold Soul--One in essence--of Man; which in the figurative language of the mystic constitutes the seven veils which conceal from (yet reveal to) Man his real Self. This concept is represented by the Rosicrucians by means of the symbol of the figure of a man surrounded by seven outlined shapes--the man, himself in his essence, is represented by the blank space disclosed by the inmost outline, and each one of the "concealing but revealing veils" is represented by an outlined figure, each being but one of the series of seven. The series of outlines, be it noted, is enclosed in the circle representing the Infinite Unmanifest.

Summary

The student must not fall into the error of supposing that man really has seven separate and distinct souls, either tied together like a bundle of twigs, or else worn as one would wear seven overcoats, one over the other. The symbol is only figurative, and must not be construed literally. There are not seven selves in man—but only One Self concealed by seven veils, each of which while serving to conceal the real nature of the Self yet serves to disclose the presence and power thereof to some degree. It is as if seven planes of variously colored glass, ranging from the darkest to the almost-transparent and colorless, were to be placed before a brilliant light. The darker glass would almost entirely obscure the Light, though yet revealing its presence in some of its rays; the next lighter would reveal more, and obscure less; and so on to the last in which the obscuration was but slight, and the revelation almost perfect. All illustrations of this ineffable fact of the Eternal are, by the very nature of things, imperfect, faulty, and misleading if taken too literally.

The lesson to the student is that in every man there lie concealed the potentiality of Godhood, and stages less than Godhood though above that of ordinary Manhood; and that in every man also abide the lower phases of manifested existence, even the very lowest of all. The wise man uses the lower, but does not allow the lower to use him; he maintains a positive, masterful mental attitude toward the lower planes of being, while opening himself receptively to the influences of the higher planes of his Self.

In conclusion, you are asked to once more consider the Seventh Aphorism: "The Soul of Man is Sevenfold, yet but One in essence: Man's spiritual Unfoldment has as its end the Discovery of Himself beneath the Seven-fold Veil."

Originally written by Magus Incognito 1918 www.magusincognito.com

Oriental Rosicrucian Success Principles with a Western Interpretation

1) Cause & Effect – Your actions and the reactions of the World": You must be aware of your choices of mind and action. With each action, you should be able to ask the following question: "What are the potential consequences of this Choice?" To begin with, constructive actions will create and build opportunity and positive outcomes. View each choice with the end result in mind. Your choices allow you to mentally visualize or feel the outcome. Therefore, you can judge the circumstance or end result in your mind's eye and in your heart. With each choice there are questions. Will it bring me peace of mind? Right action is the right response or choice for any given situation or moment. Some of us can ask our body, heart, or Spiritual center if the choice is right. Does the choice allow us to feel comfortable sensations in our Spirit? The area of the center body gives tiny emotions or feelings that will help us make decisions if we ask in mind and heart so that we can feel our inner response. With our individual journey we can have times of joy and hardship resulting from any decision. We must be able to ask ourselves what we have learned from our journey or choices. Be aware of your choices with mindfulness. Then, try and make decisions, take action, and move ahead with your journey.

2) Allow Your True Place to Appear: We must live according to providence. There are things that we are meant to do. We must dig deep into our souls to determine what our true purpose on earth is. Our being wants us to live and express our true talents and inner desires. You may have a dream to build hospitals, write poetry or create music. You may even have a calling to minister to the sick or poor. Whatever it is, be sure and express this before you leave this world. Many people find this true place in their labor. They call this a "labor of love or "right livelihood". This type of joyous work is easy and enjoyable regardless of how stressful it may be for others. This is because your purpose energizes your work and you are *having fun*.

3) Prayer, Contemplation, Meditation, Self-Evaluation: What do we want from life? We want more happiness and an ability to fulfill desires. Most of us desire abundance and a flow of goodness into our lives. In the larger scheme of life, we want and desire health and a rich life in the physical, Spiritual, and mental realms. We want peace of mind and to nurture our Spirituality. Some believe that true success is the unfolding of our Spiritual life where oneness is attained with all.

The source is the Spirit and the process is the mind. We are Spiritual mind. With the mind, we have unlimited possibilities of creative thinking. Fear and doubt is also creative but limits possibilities because it can cause paralysis in your growth. Ego and control is also a block to Spiritual growth and connection with higher powers. Real power is pure, without fear, and fueled by love. Meditation, silence, and simply being are the first and primary ways to engage and receive pure power. Non-judgment creates peace in mind. Spiritual masters often suggest that you try and not judge others just for the day in thought, word, and deed.

Further, many authors recommend meditation for thirty minutes a day, twice a day. While doing so, listen to your inner and creative thoughts and intuition that come from silence. Many teachers suggest communing with nature and becoming aware of nature. Thus, open your eyes to creation. From an internal standpoint great teachers often reveal that all external relationships are a mirror of relationship with your inner self. Therefore, it is critical to obtain inner peace so that you are at peace with others. Mastering this will allow you to respond to others with awareness and compassion. With self-realization comes wealth. What is wealth? The essence of wealth is being blessed with life energy or the Holy Spirit, and you will know it when this occurs.

4) The Law of Spiritual Detachment: Detachment and Non-resistance means to not resist moving ahead in harmony with the currents of life while maintaining and growing a sense of peace. Not allowing simple external things to hold you back. How do you achieve flow? Great teachers discuss many methods of relaxation or meditation. Men commune with nature at times to reflect on life, atone, or tune into the universal Spirit. Many Spiritual masters sincerely believe that giving attention to the "source of all" is vitally important. Further, they imply that it is highly important to develop a harmonious relationship with the Universal Spirit or Force. This can be done, of course, through the cultivation of gratitude, prayer, and meditation. Moreover, through living a life of love, tolerance, and peace, our actions will bring us closer to the source of all.

Overall, people who actively engage a Spiritual life can become very efficient and effective because they are focused and have a state of well-being. Thus, the very experienced soul can do much less work to achieve the same degree of success as the average soul. When a person is in harmony and non-resistance with the world and motivated by love and joy, life will flow to him or her with powerful rewards. Overall, the body generates and expends energy. Selfishness and the desire to control others is a great waste of precious energy. Seeking validation and approval from everyone is also a big waste of energy. Becoming who you really are is a lifelong journey. In sum, doing esteemed actions will create esteem in your life. Unfolding to your highest level will be your reward.

The Ancient Circle of Perfection of Craft Masonry

5) Some Elements of The Laws of Acceptance and Attraction:

- Acceptance of people, places, and things. Find the good in all. Develop gratitude for what is good in all things.
- Take responsibility for things as they are, and quit blaming external forces.
- Cultivate constructive thoughts and mental energy. Focus your thoughts on what you really want and *not* upon what you do not want.
- Truly feel gratitude and allow emotions of thankfulness and constructive expectation to emerge from within.
- Feel gratitude for what you desire as if you had it already.
- See in your mind's eye what you want, send it into the Universe like a letter of thanks.
- Relinquish the need to argue with others regarding your point of view. This saves and builds energy.
- Remain open minded and willing for life to unfold in abundance.
- Keep specific goals, but release your desire to control exact outcomes, because the Universe may provide a better result than you could have possibly hoped for.

6) Flow of Life and Love Energy: Giving and Receiving: Circulate your energy and Spiritual flow by giving. By giving, we receive. By doing more than the cosmos expects us to do, we are rewarded by the unbounded goodness of Karma. Give something to all persons such as the following: kind thoughts, compliments, affection, gifts of no real monetary value, compassion, radiations of your love, or bless them mentally. Giving should be unconditional without wild expectations of return of any favors or the like. Your harmonious and loving action towards others will be received and complimented in many ways. Mostly, your reward will be peace and joy, but most often, the fruits of flow come from other people who are not even related to the recipient of the initial gifts. After giving, you must be capable of receiving. Receive life's gifts and remain truly open to receive compliments, things, help, love, or even money.

7) The Manifestation of Your Dreams: Your body is part of the Universe and the Universe is an extension of your body. Both influence each other. You are connected to all through energy. Therefore, your mind and Spirit are directly linked to the world. Your consciousness allows you to effect and cooperate with the Universe. Focus your attention on what you really want from life and believe that it is possible. The quality of your focus and your intent has great power. Attention plus real burning desire allows you to forge ahead, organize plans, and complete major tasks. You must do all of this with a sense of love, thankfulness, and a desire to benefit mankind. Attention, intent, and desires should have fixity of purpose. This means to hold attention on a positive outcome. Avoid directing your attention toward your obstacles and hardships. These difficulties can be changed to opportunities if you are paying attention.

8) Some Steps to Manifesting Your Desire:

- Go into silence.
- Focus your attention upon your dreams and objectives.
- Release your carefully chosen desires.
- Don't be influenced by others' opinions, and keep your desires to yourself.
- Cultivate gratitude toward the world and allow the universe to help you.
- Relinquish attachment or anxiety toward the exact outcome.
- Allow a higher or better outcome to come into your life.
- Make a list of your desires and read them each day and night.
- Pay attention to people, places, and things that are sent to assist you in your journey.

9) The Laws of Release and Cooperation: Relinquish attachment and surrender your desires to the greater all. But, you should still maintain your desire, attention, and focus. Just continue to *send* the desire into the greater world with great faith, much like sending a mental telegram to the great force. Releasing allows you to continue to create and improve on your original desire as you go along.

There is a big materialistic flaw in this Philosophy – "When I get the next thing, I will be happy." This type of statement can be destructive because it can become a cycle of frustration, and we may never be satisfied. Thus, work hard and allow life to unfold while not being be too controlling, i.e., be flexible. In sum, allow all of the best possibilities or alternatives, and try not to force things to happen, staying alert to the options and possibilities. When you are prepared and meet the options that life gives you, this is excellent fortune.

10) Success in the Now: There is not other time but now. Your truth is what is here but sometimes beyond what you may see. We must stay aware to opportunity and possibility today. Yesterday and tomorrow cannot be acted upon today. Seek joy and happiness now. Allow your mind to engage bliss and contentment. In this day, you can do what is necessary toward your dreams and goals. However, be your best and do what you do well. As time moves forward, your harmonious actions will add up and your character will be more than it ever was. Character is the totality of your actions, thinking, omissions, and energy. If you are building character and momentum in your mind and world, other people and the Universe will instinctively know this. Therefore, your powers of attraction and usefulness to humanity will be appreciated, valued, and utilized. With your energy in the now and your consciousness directed and pointed at *growth*, you will begin to flow effortlessly with life. Provided that you maintain a sense of peace and wholeness, you will maintain a connection to the universal power. In sum, your will can fuse and be energized by the true guidance of the world.

Rosicrucians Americana - Virtues by: Benjamin Franklin

Benjamin Franklin sought to cultivate character using a methodology of thirteen virtues, which he developed at age twenty (in 1726) and continued to hone and practice his system in some form for the rest of his life. Franklin was a wise master, mystic and member of various secret esoteric lodges and societies. In 1773-74, Franklin was one of the members of the **Great or World Council of the Fraternitas Rosæ Crucis.** In 1775 Franklin was chosen a member of the Continental Congress.[xx]

1) "TEMPERANCE. Eat not to dullness; drink not to elevation."
2) "SILENCE. Speak not but what may benefit others or yourself; avoid trifling or frivolous conversation."
3) "ORDER. Let all your assets have their places; let each part of your business have its time."
4) "RESOLUTION. Resolve to perform what you must do; perform without fail what you resolve."
5) "FRUGALITY. Make no expense but to do good to others or yourself; i.e., avoid waste."

6) "INDUSTRY. Lose no time; be always employed in something useful; cut off all unnecessary actions."
7) "SINCERITY. Use no hurtful deceit; think innocently and justly, and, if you speak, speak accordingly."
8) "JUSTICE. Wrong none by doing injuries, or omitting the benefits that are your duty."
9) TRANQUILLITY. Be not disturbed at trifles, or at accidents common or unavoidable."
10) CLEANLINESS. Do not tolerate bad hygiene in body, clothes, or habitation."
11) "MODERATION. Avoid extremes; forbear resenting injuries so much as you think they deserve."
12) "CHASTITY. Rarely use venery but for health or offspring, never to dullness, weakness, or the injury of your own or another's peace and reputation."
13) "HUMILITY. Imitate Christ and Socrates. [xxi]

The Rose Croix & Rosicrucian Principles of Healing

Health & Healing Exercise

Take a time when you can have from twenty minutes to half an hour secure from interruption, and proceed first to make yourself physically comfortable. Lie at ease in a Morris chair, or on a couch, or in bed; it is best to lie flat on your back. If you have no other time, take the exercise on going to bed at night and before rising in the morning.

First let your attention travel over your body from the crown of your head to the soles of your feet, relaxing every muscle as you go. Relax completely. And next, get physical and other ills off your mind. Let the attention pass down the spinal cord and out over the nerves to the extremities, and as you do so think: - "My nerves are in perfect order all over my body. They obey my will, and I have great nerve force." Next bring your attention to the lungs and think: - "I am breathing deeply and quietly, and the air goes into every cell of my lungs, which are in perfect condition. My blood is purified and made clean." Next, to the heart: - "My heart is beating strongly and steadily, and my circulation is perfect, even to the extremities.' Next, to the digestive system: - "My stomach and bowels perform their work perfectly. My food is digested and assimilated and my body rebuilt and nourished. My liver, kidneys, and bladder each perform their several functions without pain or strain; I am perfectly well. My body is resting, my mind is quiet, and my soul is at peace.

"I have no anxiety about financial or other matters. God, who is within me, is also in all things I want, impelling them toward me; all that I want is already given to me. I have no anxiety about my health, for I am perfectly well. I have no worry or fear whatever.

"I rise above all temptation to moral evil. I cast out all greed, selfishness, and narrow personal ambition; I do not hold envy, malice, or enmity toward any living soul. I will follow no course of action which is not in accord 'with my highest ideals. I am right and I will do right."

VIEWPOINT
All is right with the world. It is perfect and advancing to completion. I will contemplate the facts of social, political, and industrial life only from this high viewpoint. Behold, it is all very good. I will see all human beings, all my acquaintances, friends, neighbors, and the members of my own household in the same way. They are all good. Nothing is wrong with the universe; nothing can be wrong but my own personal attitude, and henceforth I keep that right. My whole trust is in God.

CONSECRATION
I will obey my soul and be true to that within me that is highest. I will search within for the pure idea of right in all things, and when I find it I will express it in my outward life. I will abandon everything I have outgrown for the best I can think. I will have the highest thoughts concerning all my relationships, and my manner and action shal1 express these thought s. I surrender my body to be ruled by my mind; I yield my mind to the dominion of my soul, and I give my soul to the guidance of God.

IDENTIFICATION & RECOGNITION
There is but one substance and source, and of that I am made and with it I

am one. It is my Father; I proceeded forth and came from it. My Father and I are one, and my Father is greater than I, and I do His will. I surrender myself to conscious unity with Pure Spirit; there is but one and that one is everywhere. I am one with the Eternal Consciousness.

IDEALIZATION
Form a mental picture of your self as you want to be, and at the greatest height your imagination can picture. Dwell upon this for some little time, holding the thought: "This is what I really am; it is a picture of my own perfect and advancing to completion. I will contemplate the facts of social, political, and industrial life only from this high viewpoint. Behold, it is all very good. I will see all human beings, all my acquaintances, friends, neighbors, and the members of my own household in the same way. They are all good.

Nothing is wrong with the universe, nothing can he wrong but my own personal attitude, and henceforth I keep that right. My whole trust is in God.

REALIZATION
I appropriate to myself the power to become what I want to be, and to do what I want to do. I exercise creative energy; all the power there is, is mine. I will arise and go forth with power and perfect confidence; I will do mighty works in the strength of the Lord, my God. I will trust and not fear, for God is with me. [xxii]

- Remember that simple pains and discomforts are sometimes signals to take action to better your physical health; however, many pains are the body at work healing and regenerating itself on a cellular and molecular level.
- As a note, you may be able to work this positive person in your MIND for other people.

Rosicrucians and Mind Skills and Oriental Virtues

The Rosicrucians do a much better job than masons in instructing members on the benefits of: Goals, Desires, Visualization Exercises, Meditation etc. Generally speaking, the Orthodox Rosicrucian model is much more esoteric but also has many other practical methodologies for obtaining success and building character. The Masonic model is more like an ecumenical seminary to develop a working knowledge of metaphysical, religious and philosophical history to grow character in men. As for cause and effect, Rosicrucians place great value on observing the aspects and rules of Karma such as: Its causes, Its working out or effects, How it may be molded, The steps to be taken to be liberated from it. The great Rosicrucian Teacher Joseph Weed stated in 1941, "In considering the causes of Karma, we must first understand quite clearly that every thought, every emotion or wish and every action creates Karma. If these thoughts, ideas, desires, passions are benevolent, good Karma is created. If they are malevolent, evil Karma is created. Thus good or evil Karma attaches itself to us and remains in our life current until we have satisfied or counteracted it." Professor Weed also stated that, "Reduced to its simplest terms our duty, our dharma, is to bring light into the minds of men and love into the hearts of men." "The ways to develop the mind are many. You can study. This is natural and beneficial. You can memorize five lines or ten lines of poetry every day. This requires energy as all mental effort does but it is very rewarding. The mental nature is nourished and grows and the memory stays alive and active. But I would like to suggest a technique which everyone of you can practice with little effort and great benefit to yourself." [xxiii]

1) Meditate for ten minutes daily – no more, no less. It must be daily. Not three days a week, not just week days with Sundays and holidays excluded, but daily. Every day. And it must be meditation, which means constructive thinking and not day dreaming. The Meditation for the first year should be what is known as "meditation with seed". In other words you start with a single thought and work around it. I would suggest that you select twelve words expressive of ideals or higher emotions and use a different one as the seed thought for each month. These could be words like, "wisdom, peace, love, courage, strength, compassion, gratitude" and so forth.

2) Review your actions and decisions of the day each night. Spend not more than ten minutes each night on this. Don't become morbid or self accusing. You will probably discover plenty to find fault with if you are honest with yourself but don't waste a lot of good time on vain regrets. When you find something wrong, say to yourself – "that was a mistake – it mustn't happen again" and pass on to the next thought. If we are fair and honest in our self-appraisal, we will he able to see ourselves quite impersonally and in this manner correct our mistakes and raise the entire standard of our conduct. In addition to the raising of our vibratory rate which will coincide with the lifting of our ethical standards, this nightly resume will also lift the consciousness into the mental realm and out of the emotional. <u>A Rosicrucian Speaks, Live Lectures Published Online, Joseph J. Weed (1941-63)</u>

Rosicrucian Exercises

Concentration Exercise

1. Find a relaxed part of your home
2. Sit and quiet the mind and begin to relax each part of the body (that you can think of) from head to toes.
3. Shut your eyes & take a few deep breaths.
4. Think of a room that you lived in as a child or that you are presently in.
5. Begin to see and visualized in your mind the entire room and its contents and where things are located. (Whatever you can recall)
6. It is also good to imagine the exact color of things in the room with your eyes closed.
7. This is also a good exercise to do even after you have entered a new building or place.
8. Do this for a few minutes each day and your focus and concentration will increase. These days, there is computer software that actually runs programs to help concentration in this same way..
9. As a note, this same type of exercise is also very good to relax and vividly recall wonderful people or possessions that you have in your past or present.
- Open your eyes when done with any of these exercises ☺

Active Meditation Exercise for Intuition and Guidance

1. Engage steps 1, 2 & 3 above.
2. With eyes closed and imagining, see yourself going into a sacred castle.
3. As you enter the main chamber, you see the (helpful person of your choice).
4. This person could be alive or from the past.
5. You then discuss with her or him in your minds eye. [imagination]

6. You ask questions and your Friendly Guru answers these questions.
7. Try and sense the answers from your core (heart and stomach).
8. When you are finished, thank your friend for the help and guidance.
9. You may have an overwhelming sense that this voice or person is from a higher or different viewpoint than your own.

Exercise for Energizing or Healing Yourself.

1) Engage steps 1,2, and 3 above. (Relaxing in a chair with spine straight) relax your hands on your lap.
2) Close your eyes and visualize a peaceful lake that has no ripples. Then see yourself surrounded by bright white particles of energy that also permeates your body.
3) In your mind, see the bright light move toward and focus on the area of discomfort or pain. Allow this white light to fill any affected area and flow thought your body.
4) Know that the white light brings all of your body's healing power to work most effectively for you.
5) Take a few breaths.
6) Then, allow this bright light to act like water and flow though your body.
7) Allow the "fluid of light" purify and wash the entire body.
8) Feel and see in your minds eye that the washing fluid of white light is "pure love" and cleanses you of ANY AND ALL fear, resentment, hurt, and dis-ease.
9) Say to yourself, I forgive myself and everyone for the past. Thank the light of the universe for removing any impurities from your body.
10) Claim mental freedom from all problems in your mind and spirit. Thank the universe for your health and peace.
11) See others in your mind's eye walking up to you and congratulating you on your healing and success.
12) That's it..... & Open your eyes.

13)** To do this exercise for others, pretend that they are the person in a chair in front of you as you have your eyes closed and send a mental request of peace and health for them.

Five Exercises to Augment Peace of Mind and Mental Abilities

One: get in a quiet place where there are no distractions and think of the alphabet. Think of a letter. Select the letter "J" for instance. Think of a person in your family or in your childhood with a "J" in their name who you were very fond of or even loved. Ponder that loving emotion. Think of the happy times you had with this person. Bless that person in your mind. Consider the ability to transfer this feeling to another person in your current life.

Two:, think of a color, for example, blue. Think of something blue that you owned that gave you happiness in the past. Harvest that emotion. Feel it. Try and re-live the joy of having the thing.

Three: Consider one of the five senses (tasting, touching, smelling, hearing, seeing). Select one, such as smell. Remember your favorite aroma. Think back about the flavor or pleasant smell. Ponder the joys of enjoying that aroma again, for example, a great cup of espresso in Venice, Italy. Experience the moments in the past that you enjoyed in conjunction with the feeling and senses. Allow gratitude to fill the mind, Spirit, and body.

Four: Consider the following several methods to achieve the harmonious relationship with your world to be in tune with spiritual abundance:

- Start blessing and praising what is yours.
- Harvest a thankful heart and mind for all of your good fortune such as the ability to do simple things such as think, taste, smell, hear, see, and do, and more.
- Get into nature and wilderness to be still and feel the presence.
- Take a moment to sit or kneel and make a prayer of thanksgiving.
- Write out a list of things that you are thankful for and keep them in your wallet to read whenever you need to refocus on how you are truly blessed and protected by the Universe.
- Quit complaining and begin praising or complimenting others.
- Complement or praise somebody or a family member.
- Think of a person who was truly kind to you.
- Try and remember a person who you think really loves you.
- Think of all those who love or care for you now.
- Do something for another person to help him or her, or simply write the person a letter or give him or her a flower.
- Spend time with a spouse, loved one, or child and focus only on wonderful, beautiful, encouraging thoughts about this person.

Images copyrighted. Walter I. Anderson Bird. Est 1949?

Five: See Yourself in Your Mind's Eye

- See yourself doing what you want to do. Imagine a labor of love.
- See yourself living where you want to live.
- See yourself fulfilled in your relationships
- Act, feel, and think as if you are whom you want to be. This will assist in the growth and enhancement of your total character in reaching Spiritual abundance.

Imagine yourself in the occupation of your dreams. What would it be like? How would you feel? Harvest the emotion of having all you desire. The mind's eye is the picture screen of creation. The more clearly and powerfully you project your images in and onto your consciousness and then to your subconscious, the more easy it will be for your ideals and goals to manifest. As a secret teaching, I would imagine exactly what you want with specificity. Imagine successfully earning the best outcome. Then, I would project that image and feeling into the world, like sending out a letter. Imagine the exact completed successful outcome. You are finished and you can do this exercise later or each day until you have achieved your desire.

Perception and Awareness Exercise

1. Sit is a relaxed position
2. Relax each part of the body and take a few deep breaths.
3. Imagine a warm energy radiating through your body.
4. Enter what we call the Alpha State – which is Relaxed Daydreaming and Right Brain.
5. Now, begin to feel or sense each part of the body.
6. Direct your attention to your toes or hands or ears.
7. Notice how each part of the body feels.
8. Now close your eyes and notice any sounds either of your body or around you.
9. See if you can hear something far away.
10. Now, refocus and imagine just one sound or image.
11. Focus all of your thought on seeing, hearing, feeling, or tasting/smelling only one thing that you imagine.
12. Imagine this one thing to the exclusion of everything else.
13. As an example, try to imagine just the sound of a soft trumpet or French horn playing a song.
14. After a few minutes, relax again and come back to your BETA state of mind and consciousness. Left Brain

Affirmations and Exercises

1. Affirmations are meant to be in the affirmative. Each affirmation can be written in an "AS IF" phrase or sentence in the present tense using the "I Am or I Will" if possible. There is no need to use the "I am Not" style because negative reinforcement is not as effective as Positive Reinforcment".
2. Affirmations can be for health, success, peace, safety, relationships, or even supply in the form of money.
3. Affirmations can be said out loud or in silence. Some people love to do their affirmations in the mirror.
4. A prime example of an affirmation could be, " I am healthy, happy, successfully, loved and whole. I am part of the Supreme Intelligence and the Supreme only creates beauty and perfection."
5. Keep in mind, you should have the idea of the "essence in back of affirmations". As an example, a supply affirmation could say, "I will earn an extra 5000 dollars in the next 4 weeks by providing excellent service as a salesperson or expert or by effectively serving others...." Money is the object but the service and becoming excellence is the essence in back of the object or goal.
6. As you can see, the above affirmation specifies some distinct creative work and cooperation related to your prosperity, and it is not a blind or hopeful demand to receive something for nothing. You can always affirm mentally or out loud for possibilities and opportunities.
7. There are primary reasons against blind affirmations for things or money of which we will not discuss at length. However, if a person demands 100 thousand dollars from the supreme, it may come in the form of an injury settlement which might not be your first choice.
8. Overall, we should state our affirmations with confidence, love, harmony, gratitude, and faith. With this combination, the

universe will gladly begin working to unfold opportunities and blessings for you.
9. As such, a clear thought or idea that is repeated again and again is almost certain to manifest a replica of itself in the future. If the thought is held strongly, with gratitude and feeling, and in a creative way that does not hurt others, your desire will come quickly as the imagined formulation or something even better will unfold.

List of affirmations to improve energy, peace, and confidence.

- I am living in acceptance. I am willing to accept the best in my life.
- I will let myself enjoy the pleasures of life. I use my senses to be aware of the beauty of my surroundings. I will use my free will constructively. I will radiate love.
- I will remain open minded and this will make me more teachable.
- A good humor belongs to me. I approach life with cheer. I radiate a enthusiastic attitude to those that I care for.
- I am respectful to others and therefore, others are respectful to me.
- I have a new awareness that affords me the ability to think and be creative.
- I am a compassionate person and I am concerned about the welfare of others. Others are in turn concerned about my welfare. My service to others gives me a great release and a great strength. I serve others because I have a duty to pass on what was so freely given to me. By doing this, others are healed through the grace of the Higher Power.

- I have surrendered my reckless will to the care of my higher power. With this surrender, I have achieved a new sense of freedom and happiness. I can turn my ego over to a power greater than myself. I do not allow my ego to block me from my faith.
- I have made a commitment to my spiritual path, health, and state of mind. I am proud of my sincere commitment that I have made to the program of renewal and serenity.
- I understand that the causes of my success come from my higher power. The source of my success is by the grace of the universal spirit that flows through me.
- I radiate abundance; therefore, abundance is attracted to me. I believe in the infinite possibilities of life and success. Abundant life is a divine right and choice. Health and happiness are mine today. I do all that I need to do today, and I do not worry about tomorrow.
- I am loving and tolerant. I never know what is going on at this moment with another human being. The other person may be in the middle of a terrible situation or trauma.
- I am a responsible person. I am self-reliant. I take pleasure in being able to take care of myself and those who rely on me. I am proud to be able to do this. I receive great joy in having the ability through my Higher Power to be responsible.
- I make healthy choices. I am aware of my actions today. I make choices that I need not regret today. I receive great self-respect through my action today. My honesty and actions are good for all and good for me.
- I am forgiving. I will allow the seeds of resentment and discomfort to diffuse. I do not want to waste my time being a non-forgiving person. I have so much to do in this life without being preoccupied with non-forgiveness. I have learned a lesson, and I have moved on from the past event.
- Patience is a part of my life today. Good things will come to me in time. Opportunity is not limited, and I can be patient with regard to other people. I can also take action to accomplish my goals, but after I have done the best that I can do, I will allow the result to unfold.
- I have received the gift of spiritual strength from my Higher Power. This grace is the source of my happiness, love, and serenity.

- Today, I have the courage to speak up for myself. I do not need to live in a reactionary way; however, if there is a situation where I need to stand up for my principles, I can do so. I have the ability to say no when I need to. Further, this ability frees me from commitments that I need not participate in.
- I seek out new and different things in life. I have a sense of adventure and joy in what I do with my free time. I love life today because I view life as interesting and fun.

Image: A Mesopotamia "Wall Relief" – Louvre Museum

Twelve Meditations and Affirmations for Peace of Mind - Affirmations

Each Statement can be said silently or out loud. These meditations are designed to bring you closer to harmony with the universe, improve your self-esteem, and augment peace & abundance.

The first 12 meditations are a flowing but simple affirmation methodology to purify your mind an soul. Some people may want to go the most traditional route and read and meditate on one per day.

1st Meditation -. I surrender to the love of the Universe. I now am free to live, learn, love, laugh, and listen. I have changed and improved myself. I love and respect myself. I have stopped resisting the Supreme Spirit and now cooperate with its power, and this has given me the victory of harmonious living. Today, I will live in harmlessness. Life will unfold for constructively for me

2nd Meditation - I have serenity and peace. The Universal Spirit has granted me freedom and clarity. I am calm, relaxed, and cool. I am not in a hurry. My sense of well being keeps me in harmony with all. The universe has restored me to wholeness and satisfaction. I have all that I need for today. The Supreme Intelligence takes care of me. I am a child of God. God loves me. God is the Great Spirit that protects me.

3rd Meditation - Today, I serve the Great Spirit instead of my ego. I am connected with The Great Power. The great power gives me courage and wisdom. The great universal power is the force and source of my prosperity. Abundance is mine now. Everything I need will be provided by the abundance of the great power. I give my financial, relationship, work, family, and other issues over to the care of the Universal Spirit. I continue to do my part to be the best I can be. I am free because I release all of my problems or challenges to the power greater than myself.

4th Meditation - I work to keep a clear and free conscious. I will continue to engage in self-analysis. I will identify the good things about myself. I will also find where I have done harm or caused discomfort. I have worked to mend and clear up the past. I live a self respecting life today. I can improve and I have self-respect. I have values today that give me satisfaction because the standards that I have are good for me and all involved. I take care of myself. I make healthy decisions. Thus, I am vigorous in mind, spirit, and soul.

5th Meditation - I have discussed my past wrongs with a trusted confidant and with my higher power. I have been given great relief from working through this process of freeing my mind and forgiving myself and others. I have freed my heart and mind from the old resentments, jealously, hatred, envy, pride, greed, lust and so on. I have diffused the old negative thoughts by discussing issues with another in confidence. I have now made room for more good in my life. I am grateful for this release and this process. I am happy, enthusiastic, and energetic.

6th Meditation - I am willing to identify parts of my character that are not good for others and me. I am willing to work on improving my character and being a better person. Today, I am much better because I have lessened or eliminated some of these destructive behaviors. I am grateful that the Universal Force allows me to change for the better. My conscious connection to spirit has helped me change and improve many facets of my life. Today, I view myself as strong, vital, whole, complete, beautiful, and loving.

7th Meditation - I remember who is in charge. I am not the Supreme Master and I have learned how to co-create by cooperation. The Universe is the source of my happiness. I engage harmonious living today. I am a loving and tolerant person. I am happy because I am comfortable with myself. I take time today to be grateful for the things that I have. I have health. I have love. I care about others and myself. I remember where I came from. I am willing to be good to myself and help others today. I am strong and happy because of all of the work I have done to get where I am right now. I cooperate with the universal spirit.

8th Meditation - I live in harmony with others today. I love myself, and I radiate love because of this. I am willing to make amends to the people that I have harmed. . Today, my heart and mind are free because of my spiritual work. I feel so happy today because I have cleared a path to freedom. I am grateful that I have the tools and strategies to live a harmless and loving life. People respect and love me because I am respectful and loving. I have rebuilt many bridges, and I will create and improve relationships for the rest of my life.

9th Meditation - I am willing to apologize and forgive sincerely if needed. I admit my wrongs in my heart, mind, and in person. The recipient of my atonement at some point will understand my actions. Today, I can correct a mistake affecting another and take action to free us both of this situation.

10th Meditation - If and when I act wrongly, I will try to clean up the mess right then. I can live in harmony and humility while being a strong and intelligent person. I am stronger because I have dissolved a weakness. Today, I live in harmony. Today, I am at peace. I need not retaliate. My silence can be a skill. I can delay my reaction or retaliation. I do not need to be right all of the time. I can be a listener instead of the talker. I have a plan, and the plan will make me a greater person and give me peace.

11th Meditation - I take time to meditate. I take time for prayer. Even if it is only for one minute before I go to sleep or upon awakening. Today, I serve the will of my Universal Spirit, Higher Path and Purpose, or Supreme Power. I am connected to the source. I am now close to my Higher Power. This connection grants me strength, courage, serenity, health, love, and the ability to work hard. I can do all things through my higher power because my higher power protects and loves me.

12th Meditation - I am totally awake spiritually. I am new, and I have returned. I feel so blessed. I practice humility, gratitude, and love in my life. I try to live in harmony with all. My service to others has given me life and strength. I live a constructive and self-respecting lifestyle. I am responsible. Other people who need my help remind me of where I came from. I am grateful for these people. Today, I realize that I have received a spiritual revitalization, and I am thankful for it. I look back and identify all of the changes that I have made, and I realize the sum of the changes is the miracle of my life.

Manifesting Your Dreams – An Exercise of Realization

This is a list of Ancient Mystical, Rosicrucian and Masonic Steps for Manifestation of Goals and possibilities. Generally speaking, this is a methodological form or meditation, visualization and prayer.

- Cultivating a Peaceful Mind and Heart in Recognition of the Universal Energy
- Desire – Select an Idea that you have strong feelings about. Something that you want or need that you are willing to take action upon. i.e. a burning desire.
- Specificity, Purpose and Decision – Specifying exactly what you want. Specify pure health, peace, harmonious interactions, or specific attributes of a thing or object.
- Have it in Mind, Spirit and Mental Images – Know and see the desired outcome and results on your picture screen of your mind.
- Asking for Help/Cooperation with Spirit or Supreme Intelligence.
- Feel Unity - I AM part of and in spiritual unification with the Higher Path and Supreme. i.e You are not separate. (Can be meditations or affirmations). Knowing that you are connected allows your mental petition to be directed into the creative powers.
- Release/Send the petition to the Supreme (let it go, as you can request again anytime)
- Consecration – A surrender to the process with an affirmation of thanks and willingness.
- Willingness – Willing to do what is needed to facilitate the receipt or participate in the follow through. E.g. go to the dentist if you need to have the decay removed and a new filling inserted, or become an expert in a given field to prepare for opportunity.
- Belief and Confident Expectation – Believe that your dream, ideal, or objective is possible.
- Open your mind and heart to receiving the abundant good that the universe wants to send to you.
- Work at it while being Contemplative in Action. E.g. Go to the gym each day if you have a goal of better health or physical appearance. One thing at a time with your highest focus and concentration.
- Feel Gratitude - Thanksgiving toward the request and toward the Universe. The greater your gratitude and peace of mind, the faster the results will occur.
- This is a process that can be done in a sitting/exercise much like a meditation. *If you like, each day you can Re-affirm or even hone your objectives mentally with images, with prayer and meditation, with writing, or discussion with trusted advisor.

Things to Remember about Co-Creating and Manifesting Your Life

1. Be sure to know exactly what conditions that you wish to produce. Then analyze carefully what further results the accomplishment of your desire will lead to.
2. By letting your thought dwell upon a mental picture, you are concentrating the Creative Action of Spirit upon this desire, where mental forces are directed and expanded.
3. *Visualizing* brings your objective mind into a state of equilibrium, which enables you to consciously direct the flow of Spirit to a definitely recognized purpose, and to carefully guard your thoughts from allowing a flow in the opposite direction.
4. You must always bear in mind that you are dealing with a wonderful potential energy, which is not yet mold into any particular form, and that by the action of your mind, you can differentiate it into any specific form that you will. Your picture assists you to keep your mind fixed on the fact that the inflow of this Creative Energy is taking place. Also, by your mental picture, you are determining the direction you wish the Creative Power to take, and by doing this, you make the externalization of your picture a certainty of design.
5. Remember when you are visualizing properly that there is no strenuous effort to hold your thought-forms in place. A straining of mental effort defeats your purpose and this creates conditions that may weaken focus.
6. By holding your picture in a cheerful frame of mind, you shut out all thoughts that would disperse or dissipate the spiritual nucleus of your

picture. Because the law is Creative in its action, your pictured desire is certain of unfolding in cooperation with the Great Spirit.

7. The seventh and great thing to remember in visualizing is that you are making a mental picture for the purpose of determining the qualities that you are giving to the previously undifferentiated substance and energy, rather than to arrange the specific circumstances for its manifestation. i.e. Allow your existing idea or something even better to materialize. [xxiv]

Thoughts on Manifesting your Future and Increasing Faith

Manifestation is the work of Creative Power itself. Creation will build its own forms of expression quite naturally, if you will allow it, and save you a great deal of needless anxiety. What you really want is expansion in a certain direction, whether of health, wealth. or what not, and so long as you get it—as you surely will, if you confidently hold to your picture —what does it matter whether it reaches by some channel which you thought you could count upon, or through some other of whose existence you had no idea. You are concentrating energy of a particular kind for a particular purpose. Keep this in mind and let specific details take care of themselves, and never mention what you are doing to anyone. Remember always, that "Nature, from her clearly visible surface to her most arcane depths, is one vast storehouse of light and good entirely devoted to your individual use." Your conscious Oneness with the great Whole is the secret of success, and when you have fathomed this, you can enjoy your possession of the whole, or a part of it, at will, because by your recognition you have made it, and can increasingly make it, yours. Never forget that every physical thing, whether for you or against you, was a sustained thought before it was a thing. Thought, as thought, is neither good nor bad; it is Creative Action and always takes physical form.

Therefore, the thoughts you dwell upon become the things you possess or do not possess. BUT you ask, "How can I speak the word of Faith when I have little or no faith?" Every living thing has faith in something or somebody. Faith is that quality of Power which gives the Creative Energy a corresponding vitality, and the vitality in the word of Faith you use causes it to take corresponding physical form. Even intense fear is alive with faith. You may fear poverty and loneliness because you believe them possible for you. It is the Faith which understands that every creation had its birth in the womb of thought-words, that gives you dominion over all things, your lesser self included, and this feeling of faith is increased and intensified through observing what it does. Your constant observation should be of your state of consciousness when you did; not when you hoped you might, but feared it was too good to be true. How did you feel that time when you simply had to bring yourself into better frame of mind and did, or you had to have a certain thing and got it? Live these experiences over again and again—mentally—until you really feel in touch with the your "self" which knows and does, and then the best there is, is yours. [xxv]

"Gratitude and Thankfulness leads to greater constructive expectation in our daily living. Positive expectation and confident expectation IS FAITH. Repudiate miracles and you will receive NONE. Recognize possibility and IT WILL APPEAR. Praise others, Bless Others and Bless and Praise YOURSELF and THE MIRACLE OF YOUR CREATION. Blended with Humility, your harmonious connection to universal spirit and supply, will allow a pipeline of grace upon you. A Thankful Heart is HIGHLY conducive to Faith, Confident Expectation, and Living with JOY. Know forgiveness in your heart. Feel that the Supreme forgives you. Realize that you have forgiven all transgressions "once and for all". With your forgiveness, you free your mind's mental and spiritual power. What you think about is EXPANSIVE in your LIFE. Your focus on the good and the great will bring the good and the great into your perception and your world." [xxvi] Magus

"Being contemplative in action is the key. Having a focus and harmonious connection to the universal spirit and mind while working effectively toward your ideals, will continually reveal results. You are connected and part of all possibility. Seize upon your divine rights to supply and success. Allow yourself to be great and to do great things. There is no need to compete. YOU MUST CREATE. Create new ways of doing things, quality service, create solutions, provide opportunity and help others. Follow your true place and your dream and your talents will be exposed. If you exercise the practical steps of gratitude, faith, visualization and action, the sixth sense will emerge and you will know when to take action on ideas and fulfill them to completion." [xxvii] Magus

"Be patient and live harmoniously in a state of gratitude. The picturing of your ideals coupled with action and faith, will lead to great things. Ask and you shall receive and be ready to receive what you desire. You may have challenges or even be dealt a blow of rejection, however, universal mind allows for even bigger and better unfolding. You may not get exactly what you want, but something better may be available for your receipt and cultivation. You will be protected from bad deals and afforded opportunities for even better ones. [xxviii] Magus

Personal Magnetism

We hear much about Personal Magnetism these days. It is a peculiar quality of the mental being of the individual that serves to bring other persons into a mood or state of mind sympathetic with that of the magnetic person. Some men have this quality developed to a wonderful extent, and are able to bring about a harmonious agreement on the part of other persons in a short time, while others are almost entirely deficient in this respect and their very presence tends to arouse antagonism in the minds of others. The majority of people accept the idea of Personal Magnetism without question, but few will agree upon any theory attempting to account for it. Those who have studied the matter carefully know that the whole thing depends upon the mental states of the individual, and upon his ability to cause others to "catch" his mental vibrations. This "catching" is caused by what is known as Mental Induction. Induction, you know, is "that property or quality, or process by which one body having electrical or magnetic polarity produces it in another without direct contact. "And Mental Induction is a manifestation of similar phenomena on the mental plane. People's mental states are "catching" or "contagious," and if one infuses enough life and enthusiasm into his mental states they will affect the minds of persons with whom they come in contact.

It seems to us that the prime factor in successful Mental Induction, or manifestations of Personal Magnetism, is Enthusiasm. Enthusiasm gives Earnestness to the person, and there is no mental state so effective as

Earnestness. Earnestness makes itself felt strongly, and will often make a person give you attention in spite of himself. "It will be found that all men possessed of personal magnetism are very much in earnest. Their intense earnestness is magnetic. "And nearly every student of the subject has noted this fact. But the earnestness must be more than a firm, confident, honest belief in the thing being presented to the attention of the other person. It must be a live, contagious earnestness, which can best be described as Enthusiasm. This **Enthusiastic-Earnestness** has much emotion in it – it appeals to the Emotional side of human nature, rather that to the Thinking - Reasoning side. And yet an argument based upon reason and conducted upon logical principles, may be presented with Enthusiastic Earnestness with much greater effect than if the appeal to the reason is conducted in a cold, unemotional way. The average person is so coldly-constituted mentally that he thaws out under a manifestation of live, enthusiastic "feeling," under the term of Personal Magnetism. The "feeling" side of mentality is as important as the "thinking" side – and it is far more common and universal, for the majority of people really think very little, while everyone "feels. "   If you will notice the man and woman who are considered the most "magnetic," you will find that almost invariably they are people who have what is called "soul" about them – that is, they manifest and induce "feeling," or emotion. They manifest traits of character and nature similar to that manifested by actors and actresses. They throw out a part of themselves, which seems to affect those coming in contact with them. Notice a non-magnetic actor who is missing that "certain something," and that something may be seen to be the ability to communicate "feeling. If you will investigate the top actors, you will see that in studying their parts and practicing the same privately, these people induced a stimulated emotion, such as the part called for, and held it firmly in their minds, accompanying it with the appropriate gestures, etc. , until it became firmly "set" there – impressed upon the tablets of the mentality as the record of a phonograph is likewise impressed upon the wax.

Practitioners who seek to enhance their "attractive powers", will find it to their advantage to endeavor to work up the desired feeling of Enthusiastic-Earnestness, in private, fixing the mental impression by frequent private rehearsals and practice, until it becomes registered in their "habit mind," to be reproduced upon occasions when needed. Be a good actor – that is the advice in such cases; and remember this, that frequent practice and private rehearsal makes the good actor.

It is a far better thing to be able to induce feeling and enthusiasm in this way, rather than be lacking of it, on the one hand; or to be an "emotional inebriate" on the other hand. One may be rationally Enthusiastically-Earnest, without being filled full of overly-sentimental emotionalism. We think that the careful student will see just what is meant here, and will not misunderstand us. And remember, that through this repeated "practice" the desired quality will often become real and "natural.

As for charismatic energy, the great American author Napoleon Hill implies that we all have many forms of inner-energy which include our forces of magnetism-attraction or sexual energy. Hill's years of research of the most successful and richest persons revealed this astounding secret. Thus, concentration is critical to focus all forms of your inner energy toward your goals, influence, leadership and desires. As you know, if you are focusing your primary energies in scattered areas, you are "in essence" distracted or diffusing your power. To prevent distraction, a practitioner must be able to transmute and direct their: mental, spiritual, physical, & attraction/sexual energies.

EXERCISES

Exercise 1. Take a piece of white writing paper about six inches square, upon which you have drawn a circle about the size of a silver quarter-dollar, the circle then being filled in with black ink so that the spot will stand out black and distinct upon the white background. Pin the paper upon the wall at about the height of your eyes when are seated. Place you chair in the middle of the room and seat yourself directly facing the paper. Fix your eyes steadily upon the black spot, and gaze at it firmly, without winking, for one minute. After resting the eyes, practice the exercise again. After resting the eyes, practice the exercise again. Repeat five times. With the chair in its original place, move your paper three feet to the right of its original position. Seat yourself and fix your gaze on the wall directly in front of you, then, without moving the head, cast the eyes to the right and gaze steadily at the spot for one minute. Repeat four times. Then, placing the paper on the wall three feet to the left of its original position, gaze steadily at the spot for one minute. Repeat five times. Continue this exercise for three days, and then increase the time of the gaze to two minutes. At the end of three more days, increase the time to three minutes; and so on, increasing the time in one-minute increments every three days. Some persons have acquired the power of gazing steadily for twenty to thirty minutes, without winking or having their eyes fill with water, but I do not advise extending the limit beyond fifteen minutes. The man, who can maintain the gaze for fifteen minutes, can direct as powerful a gaze as he who has attained the thirty-minute record.

This exercise is the most important one, and, if faithfully followed up, will enable you to gaze steadily and earnestly at anyone with whom you are talking. It will impart a strong, masterful expression to the eye, and enable you to maintain a steady gaze, which few will be able to withstand. Dogs and other animals will quail before your gaze, and its effect will manifest itself also in numerous other ways. The practice of the exercises is somewhat tedious, but anyone will be amply repaid for the time and trouble bestowed upon it. If you are practicing hypnotism, you will find this gaze most helpful to you. It will have the further effect of causing the eye to appear fuller, by increasing the space between the eyelids.

Exercise 2. You may supplement the first exercise with the following, which will add variety, relieve the monotony, and accustom you to gaze into the eyes of others without embarrassment. Stand in front of your mirror and gaze into the reflection of your own eyes, in the manner mentioned in Exercise No. 1. Increase the time as in the previous exercise. This exercise will accustom you to bear the gaze of others, and also will enable you to obtain the best expression of the eye, and in other ways will be useful to you. It will enable you to see the growth and development of the characteristic expression of your eye when it is acquiring the magnetic gaze. By all means practice this exercise, systematically. Some authorities prefer this exercise to the preceding one, but, in my opinion, the best results are obtained by a combination of the two.

Exercise 3. Stand erect, facing the wall at a distance of three feet. Place your sheet of paper in front of you, with the spot directly in front of the eyes. Fix your gaze upon the spot, and then move your head around in a circle, keeping your gaze fixed upon the spot. As this exercise causes the eyes to roll around and keeping the gaze steady, the nerves and muscles receive considerable exercise. Vary the exercise by circling the head in different directions. Use the exercise mildly at first, and avoid tiring the eyes.

Exercise 4. Stand with you back against the wall, and, facing toward the opposite wall, shift your gaze rapidly from one point of the wall to another - right, left, up, down, zigzag, circle, etc. This exercise should be discontinued when the eyes begin to feel tired, the best plan for concluding the exercise being to gaze intently at one point, which will rest the eyes after the previous motion. This exercise is calculated to strengthen the muscles and nerves of the eye.

Exercise 5. After having acquired a firm gaze, you will gain confidence by persuading a friend to allow you to practice your gaze upon him. Place your friend in a chair opposite your own; sit down and gaze calmly, steadily and firmly into his eyes, instructing him to look at you as long as he can. You will find that you will easily tire him out, and that by the time he cries "enough" he will be in an almost hypnotic condition. If you have a hypnotic subject, he (or she) will answer still better. You also may try the strength of your gaze on a dog, cat or other animal, provided that you are able to induce it to stand still or lie still. You will find, however, that most animals will move away, or turn the head, in order to avoid you steady gaze.

You of course will distinguish between a steady, calm gaze, and an impudent stare. The first is indicative of the man of strong psychical power whilst the latter denotes the cad.
You will find, at first, that your strong, steady gaze may somewhat disconcert those with whom you come in contact, and may embarrass those at whom you are directing your gaze, causing them to become uneasy and "rattled" You will soon accustom yourself to your new power, and will use it discreetly, so as to avoid embarrassment to others whilst producing an effect on them.   I would caution you against discussing or speaking of your eye exercises, or practice of Personal Magnetism, to

others, as that course would result only in making people suspicious of you, and in other ways proving a serious detriment to the proper use of your powers of influencing people. Keep your own secrets, and let your force manifest itself by results, not by boasting. In addition to these reasons, there are good occult reasons why you should keep your own council about your new accomplishments. A neglect to observe this advice will be a source of regret to you. Take your time in practicing these exercises, and do not rush things unduly. Follow Nature's rule and develop your power gradually but surely. [xxix]

Cycles of Life

There are many mystics historically involved with Rocrucianism that have advocated the cycles of life theories and methods. One could speculate that it is based on astrology, but it is more founded on your birthday, life growth, and your life span.   As such, Man is purported to be designed to live 140 years with cyclic periods of 7 years each. We have discovered that the particles of our bodies are constantly changing; that at least once in seven years there is a change in every atom of matter composing them. Thus, in the first 3 periods of 7 years, each person is growing, maturing and developing physically, mentally, and spiritually. From 21 to 28 and then to 35, persons are also developing skill, mastery and other wisdom. By the time we are 42 years old, we have had ample time to become alchemists and magi over our destiny if we have embraced certain virtues and metaphysical laws. Below is a list of 7 periods of the year after your birthday. The year starts with your birthday and goes forward 52 days. The year is comprised of 7 periods of 52 days. Each person can calculate their own 7 yearly periods.

1	Period	Opportunity, Ask For Favors, Seek Jobs
2	Period	Travel, Short Projects, No Big Changes
3	Period	Energized, Compete, Stamina
4	Period	Mental, Imagination, Creative, Spiritual

5	Period	Can Achieve Great Success, Receive
6	Period	Relaxation. Rest, Holiday Time
7	Period	Catharsis, Attone, Growth, New Cycle

We will leave these words and periods above to your imagination. The metaphysical rule is that we should continually grow and engage action in each season and period of the year. Further, don't let these periods distract you. They are merely a guide for each year to: Grow, Change, Rest, Reflect, Engage Life, See the beauty of the world and much more.

7 Levels of Metaphysical Development of the Spiritual Seeker – Laws of Seven.

1. Raw Form
2. A model or form (physical component)
3. The Breath of Life or Thought – Spark of Creation
4. Desire or Impelling force of Thought and Will
5. Ego thought consciousness (Needs to be refined)
6. To awaken, enlighten, know i.e. Refined Thinking
7. The seventh is called Atman (Sanskrit). Pure consciousness. It is the feeling and knowledge of "I am," pure thought and cognition/mind.

This analysis above also applies to the 7 stages of growth of man. Each of us has cycles which easily correlate to our growth, puberty, manhood/womanhood, intelligence and wisdom development.

Philosophy of Harmony and Gratitude

To convey the idea of your wants to the universe, it becomes necessary to relate yourself to the formless intelligence in a harmonious way. To have a harmonious relationship with the cosmic is to develop a command and true communication with the supreme elements. To secure this harmonious relation is a matter of such primary and vital importance that I shall give some space to its discussion here and give you instructions which, if you will follow them, will be certain to bring you into perfect unity of mind with the Supreme Power, or God. The whole process of mental adjustment and attunement can be summed up in one word: Gratitude.

First, you believe that there is one intelligent substance, from which all things proceed. Second, you believe that this substance gives you everything you desire. And third, you relate yourself to it by a feeling of deep and profound gratitude. Many people who order their lives rightly in all other ways are kept in poverty by their lack of gratitude. Having received one gift from God, they cut the wires which connect them with the Supreme by failing to make acknowledgment.

It is easy to understand that the nearer we live to the source of wealth, the more wealth we shall receive, and it is easy also to understand that the soul that is always grateful lives in closer touch with God than the one which never looks to the SUPREME in thankful acknowledgment. The more gratefully we fix our minds on the supreme when good things come to us, the more good things we will receive, and the more rapidly they will come. And the reason simply is that the mental attitude of gratitude draws the mind into closer touch with the source from which the blessings come.

If it is a new thought to you that gratitude brings your whole mind into closer harmony with the creative energies of the universe, consider it well, and you will see that it is true. The good things you have already have come to you along the line of obedience to certain laws. Gratitude will lead your mind out along the ways by which things come, and it will keep you in close harmony with creative thought and prevent you from falling into competitive thought. Gratitude alone can keep you looking toward the all, and prevent you from falling into the error of thinking of the supply as limited — and to do that would be fatal to your hopes.

There is a law of gratitude, and it is absolutely necessary that you should observe the law if you are to get the results you seek. The law of gratitude is the natural principle that action and reaction are always equal and in opposite directions. The grateful outreaching of your mind in thankful praise to the Supreme intelligence is a liberation or expenditure of force. It cannot fail to reach that to which it addressed, and the reaction is an instantaneous movement toward you.

"Draw nigh unto God, and he will draw nigh unto you." That is a statement of psychological truth. And if your gratitude is strong and constant, the reaction in formless substance will be strong and continuous; the movement of the things you want will be always toward you. Notice the grateful attitude that Jesus took, how he always seems to be saying, "I thank thee, Father, that thou hearest me." You cannot exercise much power without gratitude, for it is gratitude that keeps you connected with power. But the value of gratitude does not consist solely in getting you more blessings in the future. Without gratitude you cannot long keep from dissatisfied thought regarding things as they are.

The moment you permit your mind to dwell with dissatisfaction upon things as they are, you begin to lose ground. You fix attention upon the common, the ordinary, the poor, the squalid, and the mean — and your mind takes the form of these things. Then you will transmit these forms or mental images to the formless. And the common, the poor, the squalid, and the mean will come to you.

To permit your mind to dwell upon the inferior is to become inferior and to surround yourself with inferior things. On the other hand, to fix your attention on the best is to surround yourself with the best, and to become the best. The creative power within us makes us into the image of that to which we give our attention. We are of thinking substance, too, and thinking substance always takes the form of that which it thinks about.

The grateful mind is constantly fixed upon the best. Therefore it tends to become the best. It takes the form or character of the best, and will receive the best. Also, faith is born of gratitude. The grateful mind continually expects good things, and expectation becomes faith. The reaction of gratitude upon one's own mind produces faith, and every outgoing wave of grateful thanksgiving increases faith. The person who has no feeling of gratitude cannot long retain a living faith, and without a living faith you cannot attain true prosperity by the creative method.

It is necessary, then, to cultivate the habit of being grateful for every good thing that comes to you and to give thanks continuously. And because all things have contributed to your advancement, you should include all things in your gratitude. Do not waste a lot of time thinking or talking about the shortcomings or wrong actions of those in power. Their organization of the world has created your opportunity; all you get really comes to you because of them. Do not rage against corrupt politicians. If it were not for politicians we should fall into anarchy and your opportunity would be greatly lessened.

The Supreme Intelligence has worked a long time and very patiently to bring us up to where we are in industry and government, and he is going right on with his work. There is not the least doubt that he will do away with plutocrats, trust magnates, captains of industry, and politicians as soon as they can be spared, but in the meantime, they are all very necessary. Remember that they are all helping to arrange the lines of transmission along which your riches will come to you, and be grateful. This will bring you into harmonious relations with the good in everything, and the good in everything will move toward you. xxx

The Philosophy of Wealth

There is a spiritual energy and force in every thought, from which all things are made, and which, in its original state, permeates, penetrates, and fills the interspaces of the Universe. A thought in this substance produces the thing that is imaged by the thought. Persons can form things in their thought, and by impressing their thoughts upon formless substance (interspaces of the Universe) can cause the thing he they think about to be created. In order to do this, people must pass from the competitive to the creative mind. Otherwise they cannot be in harmony with formless intelligence, which is always creative and never competitive in Spirit. *i.e.*

Being for the Creation of something and against nothing. People may come into full harmony with the formless substance by entertaining a lively and sincere gratitude for the blessings it bestows upon them. Gratitude unifies the mind of man with the intelligence of substance, so that man's thoughts are received by the formless. People can remain upon the creative plane only by uniting themselves with the formless intelligence through a deep and continuous feeling of gratitude. People must form a clear and definite mental image of the things they want to have, to do, or to become, and they must hold this mental image in their thoughts while being deeply grateful to the supreme that all their desires are granted. People who desire abundance must spend their leisure hours in contemplating their vision, and in earnest thanksgiving that the reality is being given to them. Too much stress cannot be laid on the importance of frequent contemplation of the mental image, coupled with unwavering faith and devout gratitude. This is the process by which the impression is given to the formless and the creative forces set in motion. The clear and defined image can be sent into the universe as a confident petition for help. We should know how we will use the resulting abundance and understand the essence of how the prosperity will be used.

The creative energy works through the established channels of natural growth, and of the industrial and social order. All that is included in his mental image will surely be brought to people who follow the instructions given above, and whose faith does not waver. What they want will come to them through the ways of established trade and commerce. In order to receive their supply when it is ready to come to them, people must be in action in a way that causes them to more than fill their present place. They must keep in mind the clear purpose of prosperity through emotionalized realization of their mental image. And they must do, every day, all which can be done that day, taking care to do each act in a successful manner. They must give to every person a use value in excess of the value they receive, so that each transaction makes for more life, and they must hold the advancing thought so that the impression of increase will be communicated to all with whom they comes into contact. The men and women who practice the foregoing instructions will certainly achieve abundance, and the riches they receive will be in exact proportion to the definiteness of their vision, the fixity of their purpose, the steadiness of their faith, and the depth of their gratitude.[xxxi]

The Philosophy of Greatness

We are made of the one intelligent substance, and therefore all contain the same essential powers and possibilities. Greatness is equally inherent each unique individual, and may be manifested by all. Every person may become great. Many of the highest constituents of the Supreme Intelligence are also the constituents of man. We must learn to tap into these unused and latent spiritual powers.

We may overcome both heredity and circumstances by exercising the inherent creative power of the soul. If we are to become great, the soul must act, and must rule the mind and the body over the simple ego thoughts. Our knowledge is limited, and we fall into error through spiritual ignorance. To avoid this illusion and unawareness, we must connect our soul with Universal Spirit. Universal Spirit is the intelligent substance from which all things come. It is in and through all things. All things are known to this universal mind, and we can so unite ourselves with it as to enter into spirit and higher knowledge. To do this we must cast out of ourselves everything that separates us from the Supreme. We must have sheer willingness to live the divine and abundant life, and we must rise above all simple, trivial, & moral temptations. The seeker of spiritual abundance must forsake, repudiate, or transcend every course of action that is not in accord with our highest ideals. We must reach the right viewpoint, recognizing that God is all, in all, and that there is nothing wrong. We must see that nature, society, government, and industry are perfect in their present stage, and advancing toward completion; and that all men and women everywhere are good and perfect while each on their own journey.

We must know that all is right with OUR world, and unite with the Supreme for the engagement of perfect expression & work. It is only as we see the Universal Spirit as the Great Advancing Presence in all and see the good in all, that we can shift our consciousness to real greatness. The seeker must consecrate themselves to the service of the highest that is within, obeying the voice of their heart and spirit. There is an Inner Light in everyone that continuously impels us toward the highest, and we must be guided by this light if we would become great. We must recognize the fact that we are one with the Supreme, and consciously affirm this unity for ourselves and for all others. We must know ourselves to be a "child of God" among "children of God", and act accordingly. We must have absolute faith in our own perceptions of truth, and begin at home to act upon these perceptions. As we see the true and right course in small things and actions, we must take that course. We must cease to act unthinkingly, and begin to think; and we must be sincere and honest in our thought. We must form a mental conception of ourselves at the highest, and hold this conception until it is our habitual thought-form of ourselves. This thought-form we must keep continuously in view. We must outwardly realize and express that thought-form in our actions. We must do everything that we do in a great way. In dealing with our family, neighbors, acquaintances, and friends, we must make every act an expression of our ideals or highest good. The person who reaches the right viewpoint and makes this full consecration, and who fully idealizes their self as great, and who makes every act, however trivial, an expression of the ideal, has already attained to greatness. Everything we do will be done in a great way. We will inherently make ourselves known by our good work and thinking, and will be recognized as a personality of power. We will receive knowledge by inspiration, and will know all that we need to know. We will benefit from and receive all the wealth we form in our thoughts, and will not lack for any good thing. We will be given ability to deal with any combination of circumstances that may arise, and our growth and progress will be continuous and rapid. [xxxii]

Harmony and Creation

We should cultivate this habit in moments of mediation, when we may escape from the people and crowd, and thus be able to listen to the voice that sounds from within. Here are a few directions for entering into harmony with the Universal Rhythm of Force; First, your mental attitude must be right. You must have gained control of your thoughts and words, so that your mind is open and receptive to the great good of the world. There must be no hate there, no discouragement, no pessimism, no negative, cringing, worm-of-the-dust or poverty thought—your frame of mind must be that of good will, encouragement, optimism, with positive thoughts, expectant of wealth, prosperity, and all of the good things that a person should have as an heir of the universe. This constructive and peaceful mental attitude will surround you with a personal thought atmosphere which repels from you the negative or toxic things and attracts you to the positive or good energy from the world.

Early in the morning just after your bath, close the doors of your room, shutting out everybody and everything for just a few moments. Take precautions that you shall not be disturbed, and put away from your mind the fear of interruption and disturbance. Take a position of restful and peaceful calm. Relax every muscle, and take the tension off every nerve. Take a few deep restful breaths which will seem like sighs, and will tend to relax your body and mind. Then detach your thoughts from the outer world, the things, and turn the mind inward upon yourself. Shut out all the material cares, worries and problems of the day, and sink into a mental state of a peaceful calm. Think "*I open myself to the inflow of the universal rhythmic harmony,*" and you will soon begin to feel a sense of relationship with that harmony coming into you, filling your mind and body with a feeling of rest and peace, and latent power. Then shortly after will come to you a sense of new strength and energy, and a desire to once more emerge upon the scene of your duties. This is the time for you to close your meditation.

Here it is; a few moments spent with your inner self and the Great Universal Power each day, as described above, if practiced assiduously, will establish within you the Creative Mind—that wonderful thing which marks the difference between the miserable realist who is determined to be right about 'all that is wrong" and the master of destiny to refuses to view the world through anything but rose colored glasses. The more you practice, the more you will open up that great subconscious reservoir of yours which is overflowing with original ideas. In time you will gain the power to get in touch with your inner self and tap that reservoir where ever you may be—in a car—out for a walk—while you are shaving—and there will be a flash through to your subconscious mind, in vivid outlines, ideas that when worked out will mean for you prosperity and independence.

Teachings and Strategies of Spiritual Growth

- Are you willing to have a better life. Are you tired and ready for improvement. Then, you must find a way to achieve a higher harmony with the world, yourself, and your Higher Power. Once you have cleared a path for a new life through atonement and attunement, you become ready to engage the journey of life with a new awareness, strength, and energy.
- After you have reshaped the cornerstone of your life, then you must be ready to learn the spiritual strategies of abundant life. The activity of life usually involves doing things efficiently and effectively.   If you can complete one task at a time and finish it, you will always move forward. Because over time, you will pile up tiny successes into a richer and fuller life, one day at a time. How do you achieve little tasks? You think the thought, your thought turns to desire, your desire becomes a plan, you make a blueprint, you familiarize yourself with what it takes to accomplish the plan, and you begin to implement the plan with a vision of purpose and completeness.
- Each task or plan must be done. We must become proactive and complete these tiny tasks. We must pick up the phone, get out of the house, build that relationship, and so on. If the task is not fulfilled, then we were protected for a bad situation, and we have something better on the way.
- As we have entered into the next level or phase of spirituality, we do not want to enter relationships where both parties do not benefit. We can always work and live in situations where we can give and receive.

Remember, what you do or sell may be of great benefit to others and never devalue it. If it is too competitive and stressful, you may seek out a better way to achieve your aspirations.
- Your Higher Power is the source of all of your good that flows within you and you do not need to tell others of your spiritual path and learning of spiritual laws.
- Believe that God will fulfill all of your needs with prosperity and do not limit or resist God and the spirit within you. Seek daily to improve your connection with the spirit within using gratitude toward it. Your gratitude toward your inner and outer Higher Power will flow back to you in great abundance.
- Make sure that your desire is something that you are willing to focus upon and do what it takes to achieve. You must be creative and not just competitive. Mentally visualize your possibilities in the highest form. See as vivid as possible on a daily basis how your true aspirations will take shape. Feel in your heart and mind that they are happening and even already materialized.
- Develop clarity and a specific desire. Mentally define in your minds eye and on paper what your desire looks like, the images, colors and sounds of the end result, when it will happen, and feel as though you have it now. Imagine yourself enjoying the complete result. Thoughts will transform into real things with the proper desire, faith, gratitude, and spiritual nature. Also, spend time imagining who you intend to become and your characteristics including self-confidence.
- Seek advice and counsel of those who will encourage you. This will allow you to hone your ideas and act as a guide to your decisions.
- Limit or remove the unhealthy choices in your life and detach from greed, lust, anger, resentment, blame, frustration, ego etc. and work to purge all negativity from you mind. Mentally exercise and change your thinking through gratitude, love consciousness, a thankful heart, and acceptance.
- Surrender control of the people, places, things, outcomes, and expectations. You are not trying to force any specific outcome... it will unfold for you. Don't forget that you should not give others free rent in your mind. The world is waiting for us to become what we are supposed to be, and we have to allow it to happen.

- You must be specific about your goals and objects but detach from absolute results while turning your objectives over to the universe. But, you must condition the mind to cooperate with divine direction and guidance.
- Realize that it is your divine right to be rich in life, love, health, joy, and success and your highest desires can manifest in the present as long as you are willing to receive it and believe that it is possible.
- Realize that wealth, success, joy, and health are yours for the asking. Open you mind to it and be willing to accept the best in all of these categories. It is right for you to expect the best combination of mind, body, and spiritual development
- We are spiritual bodies living in a human world. Therefore, we must abide by spiritual laws and grow at that level over time. If we continually deny our spiritual nature, we may remain in conflict with ourselves by resisting the inner source of peace, harmony, and prosperity.
- Continue to surround yourself with those seeking spiritual growth. Continue to refresh and rebuild your mind through exercises of steps. Continue to seek counsel, companionship, and conversation with spirit minded individuals. The reason you do this is that the insight form others is flowing from divine sources. The insight is from people who are operating from a similar spiritual plane as you.
- Visualize your life and aspirations with completeness, finality, faith, and wholeness.
- Renew your focus mentally each day and remain grateful and accepting of the best for you. The biggest limitation to you is your state of mind. Keep it conditioned for success, peace, and satisfaction.
- Before you can have desire you must think. Your thinking is important because it is what ties you to the world. Your actions and creativity is based on thought. How do you think? Are you strictly impulsive? The question here is do you use exercises to induce thinking? Do you allow harmony with higher self to facilitate intuitive thinking. There are several ways to do this but we must focus on several issues. First, we need time in silence and time for silence of mind. These moments free up the reception of thought from the other parts of your mind. Thus, you can receive that divine thinking that is precious and positive in your life. This is a form of meditation. Moreover, these times of thoughtful review are most fruitful when your state of mind is free of resentment, judging, and anxiety. To enter this phase when you are not in a good state of mind,

you can either sit down and take a few deep breaths or do some exercises and then you can lie down and rest.
- You will become more conscious of your actions toward yourself and others. Over time, you will be more concerned about what you say or do to others. You can become more skillful in what you say and more tactful in the ways that you act. All of this will be in line with doing the right thing and good orderly direction. Self respect is built in this process. Further, you will be attracting good action toward you by others. This is in line with the golden rule and if we act in an excellent way to others, we will be treated this way over time.
- Remember to act in harmlessness. Act in harmony with the world. You can enter a state of mind that the world is helping you and you are cooperating with it. Accept responsibility for your actions. Continue to move forward with your ideas, work, relationships and endeavors. You do not need to coerce anyone to do anything.
- You can prepare, plan, think intuitively, and relate what you want to the universe through a grateful heart and action. You do not need to be adversely effected by others. You should accept the situation and keep moving ahead with your spiritual path. When you are in the flow of life, you can work in an effortless fashion and get many things completed in a successful way.

- Throughout all of this, you are finding your highest self and tuning into the spiritual power that you have neglected. You are awakening your spirit, mind, body, and soul. You are developing a renewed faith and gratitude for life. Your goals include finding out your true talents and skills. You may find that you have hidden talents with music, writing, analysis, teaching, etc. Overall, your career, spiritual life, and talents will be found at a new and deeper level because it is part of the spiritual path to success. As we have mentioned before, all of us have a purpose. Your purpose can be found and developed through journaling, discussing your aspirations with others, and working to improve your life and connection with the spirit.
- Don't fall back into to the ego. Your self seeking will change into a new type of self seeking that is good for all. You will find that you are pleased with your new self honesty, and this honesty allows you to improve your life and have greater direction. Try and purge the blaming frame of mind. Remember, "Life is very fair because life can be unfair to everybody"

- Giving of service and love is a huge concept. I think some relationships can last forever if you always give more than you receive without expectation of a payback. Naturally, this works best when the other person in the relationship has some awareness of how much you do to support and love them. It does not take fancy gifts to impress people. I have always appreciated a handwritten card over a small gift. Or, if you visit somebody you care about, you can bring them a small gift such as a book, some candy, or a flower
- Freeing yourself from the bondage of the world is another positive exercise. Sometimes, I refuse to read the local newspaper so I can avoid the affect of this type of exposure. I chose what I read carefully. I chose what I talk about with prudence. This is not avoiding challenges but merely limiting toxic exposures from venues that you know are not the proprietors of spiritual truth.
- When you are in tune with the spirit, you will be able to flow with your intuition that comes from that great force. Your reasonable desires and goals can manifest in proper time according to the will of your higher power.

Here are some steps that most people may find necessary to change, grow or even heal.

1. A burning desire supported by real facts.
2. Repairing error thought – incorrect human beliefs about self and others.
3. Writing out or discussing what you really want to do with your life.
4. Humility and a willingness to listen and learn (teach-ability)
5. Ability to rise above the challenges & to forgive self and others
6. An ability to do what it takes to transcend above challenges.
7. A clear comprehension of the benefits of change, the sacrifices needed to transcend, and the pain associated lack of change.
8. Moving toward Natural Expression of what your life was meant to be.

Some Related Thoughts:

- What is the reality of our situation? Is the situation after we have begun our abundant path improving? What is the truth? The truth of the matter is that you are probably doing 10 times better than you think. Never let your mind play tricks on you. You are progressing, and you have the ability to be a better person.
- Right thinking, keeping a pure heart, remaining focused away from desire and ego. Doing what needs to be done and not procrastinating.
- Tame our speech, gossip, criticism of the government, and frivolous talk. We may just be better off listening instead of talking all of the time.
- Guard our actions and omissions. If we are still acting our of our old behavior, we have much work to do. The good news is that we have the rest of our lives to live in sobriety, and we can learn to be good to ourselves and to others.
- Approach most of life with some type of moderation. After a while, we will be able to notice when we become so preoccupied with something that it is consuming our serenity.
- The flip side of our overdoing something can be not doing enough. Over time, we will find ourselves weak in areas that we would prefer to excel in. We can use our frustration or anger in these situations to move on and change focus or we can double our efforts or simply become more focused on what is necessary and what is a waste of our time.
- We should keep a balanced state of mind and remain open to change or evolution in our souls, bodies, and minds.
- Further, we should find quiet time for ourselves to go deep inside to listen to our higher self, higher power, and intuition. This is part of our maintenance and daily atonement.

Rosy Cross Americana – A Summary of Effective Metaphysics

It is arguable that the definition of abundance is the quality of freedom and prosperity necessary for you to advance in the direction of your dreams and potential to attain your fullest mental, Spiritual, and physical prosperity. You have a right to affluence because it is simply a desire for you to have a richer, fuller, and more abundant life of health, happiness, faith, knowledge, or even wealth. We all should live for the equal advancement and fulfillment of body, mind, and soul, and there is no reason we should limit our capacities in any of the three sectors. Many people see greed, lust, and arrogance in the rich, and wonder if any wealthy people are truly happy. Ironically, poverty can and will frustrate your relationship with Spirit and people, especially with those you love. Further, mental poverty creates a negative self-esteem, confidence, and outlook upon life. With poverty of mind and life, you may have nothing to give to those you love and care about, which leads to a very limited life and ability to connect to people and the world. Remember, giving is a form of love and compassion. In sum, abundance and wealth are the same, and if we recognize it and get in tune with it, prosperity will show itself in each of our lives.

If you are complacent with your life, then this book is not for you. Stay where you are. Do not advance. Do not exercise your talents to the fullest. Do not leave your gift, mark, or legacy to the world in the form of improvements, opportunity, or education for all. However, if you want more out of life, and you are tired of failure, we will give you the secrets to success and the keys to prosperity. Why would or should you sit idly by and reject of deny the abundance of the world when it awaits your cooperation and seeking. The world is plentiful with resources, and your creativity is one of the many secrets to your future success. You do not need money to start something, to plan, to begin. You do not need a special talent or to save every penny to be rich and abundant in life. You do not need the perfect business location for your offices. Many people become wealthy with no talent, no college education, a less than perfect place to work and live, and no start-up capital. The time is now to change your mind about life and to begin anew. When you are ready and willing to change and open your heart and mind, the gold mine of abundance will be available to you. The whole world of past and present has its eyes on you, waiting for you to achieve your dreams, and all you need to do is make the mental and Spiritual shift in consciousness.

There is plenty of opportunity, health, and success. Creativity, innovation, and abundance will go to the people who flow and cooperate with life and not reject it. Nature has an inexhaustible source of riches. Accordingly, it is natural to seek more from life, and your advancement is vital for growth. As the old adage states, "We grow or die." On the higher plane and dimension, a person can make forty years worth of advances in three to six years with efficient work. For example, the last one-hundred years has shown more life and technological improvements than the last two-thousand years of civilization. We will now show you the first secret of life. This key to success can be yours if you simply accept the following statement. Just take it as fact, and the world will begin to move with you.

THOUGHT PRECEEDS FORM

You conceive of your desire, you believe that your goal will happen, and you retrieve the opportunity from the world's storehouse of riches and beauty. As a rule, man originates thought. Thought turns into plans or mental images in the mind. Man can communicate his thought and mental images into and throughout the world. This creation begins with our thought focused within and without. Your mind is the center of your world. The presence of the universal Spirit can be allowed into your mind.
Your thoughts mixed with a thankful heart directed toward your inner presence can flow out into the world. You picture and believe that your healthy goal is possible. You understand the essence and reasons that you should have this type of result in your life. You picture your goal with specificity. You think of and picture the opportunity frequently. You believe that you have the type of result that you desire. You feel it and harvest the emotion of having it as much as possible. [xxxiii]

These thoughts and a mental practice of visualization will be sent off into the world like a letter of request. If you practice this visualization enough, the desires you have will be met. Truth is your faithful non-doubting interpretation of your thoughts. Do not focus on failure, poverty, disease, or lack. Your truth is health, riches, success, and happiness. Do not doubt your thoughts and dreams. Do not speak against them. Keep these mental petitions as faithful as possible while living harmoniously with people, places, institutions, and the Universe.

It is the desire of the universal Spirit that you should have all that you need. You will begin with a simple desire for some type of improvement in life. A desire coupled with unwavering faith will correctly unfold for you over time. The motives of your desires are important: You want to help yourself and others, and you do not want to hurt other people.

You will achieve these desires much more quickly if your motives are not colored with greed, ego, pride, lust, competition, hate, resentment, and arrogance. Your desires must be propelled by love, gratitude, faith, confidence, mental focus, truth, acceptance, creativity, positive expectation, clear planning, and the giving of more love and value than you take.

TO BEGIN YOUR PROCESS OF PROSPERITY

Brainstorm on your ideas each day. Clarify in you mind exactly what you want and how you will achieve it. Hold the picture of the moment you have completed the achievement with positive certainty. Never speak or think of it as not being possible. Claim it as yours, claim the picture of success as a "FACT" and that it is already yours in mind. Keep your mind tuned in to the universal presence and energy by having a thankful heart and grateful thoughts. If you can not be grateful, then, begin to think of your ability to walk, talk, see, hear, travel, speak, etc. The simplest of freedoms to be grateful for are the most easily overlooked. But, these abilities such as your health are the quickest way to show gratitude and begin a new and powerful positive outlook that connects you to life and your dreams. People will soon not recognize your new outlook and serenity. Remember, that you must exercise this mental picturing and thankfulness every day for at least a month. However, after a month, you will not believe the difference

in your perception of life. Do not be frightened or ashamed to ask for what you really want. Ask for more than you need.
The world is full of people to give and receive. Never be frightened to receive. Receive with humility, thankfulness, and appreciation. Extreme poverty and self-sacrifice are not pleasing to anyone, and extreme altruism is just as dangerous as extreme greed or piety. Thus, give and receive with joy.

We believe that there is a universal Spirit of which unlimited abundance flows. It will give us all that we need and desire when we have a pure heart. A pure heart and mind simply means that you do not allow the weeds of ignorance, bitterness, hate, and irritation to cloud and fill your mind. To facilitate a mind of purity, we make the profound connection to the universal Spirit within us by developing a strong feeling of thankfulness for life, love, health, and our material gifts that we already have or will have. Let us think about gratitude and thankfulness. Can you have happiness with a bitter heart? Can you have real faith when you are constantly blaming, angry, and ungrateful? If you think you can be happy with a blaming, hateful, and bitter mind, then, good luck. If you want to change to an outlook on life where you feel that all is possible, then keep reading.

Think back and reflect on the times in your life when you got what you wanted and became arrogant or ego centered. After you got what you wanted or got out of a jam, you forgot about and abandoned your connection to your universal Spirit. You may have given up your connection to the Spirit and world because you thought you had won the game of life. When good things happen to you is the *exact* time that you should exercise and practice having grateful thoughts to continue the flow of abundance and riches to us. What you focus on expands. What becomes important to you will come to you and remain with you. If you have doubt and fear, your gratitude will dispel fear and doubt. Gratitude will keep you connected to the world and affords you a harmonious relationship with all. Gratitude and thankfulness prevent dissatisfaction. Continue to fix your attention on thanks and the best in life. Fix you mind on health, love, success, and good fortune.

Your faith will be renewed and strengthened from your exercise of gratitude. It may not happen overnight, but within a month of this simple five-minute-a-day practice, you *will* have results. As an exercise, go a week without complaining.

As you may know, complaining attracts destructive people, places, and things into your life. Each time you find yourself complaining, touch each of your shoulders with your finger, and proclaim, "I am abundance." If you have trouble with certain negative triggers, then eliminate them. If government bothers you, then quit reading the paper for a while. If certain people constantly annoy you, then you should avoid them for a time too. You are working on yourself, and it is OK to take care of your well-being first. The people around you will be happy in the end, if you rebuild and renew your positive Spirit and enthusiasm for life as a priority. This is putting your health first, i.e., your Spiritual health. Your desires should be very specific. Your mental blueprint must be just as precise. For example, you may write out on a piece of paper a personal contract to yourself:

I, John Doe, Jr., will have (a successful venture worth XXX dollars) XXX years from today. I will sell creative *widgets*. I will give the best service and value to my clients. My products and services will have outstanding benefits and will help all of my customers. I will do all of these things, work hard, and be persistent in my service and quality. I will not give up. People will be glad to pay me for my services because they are a benefit to the customer. I will gladly accept payment and do what I need to do to receive the compensation.

Jan. 1, XXXX , John Doe, Jr.
SIGNATURE

Spend each day contemplating your personal contract. Visualize the million-dollar business. Form a mental image of you being paid one million dollars for the business in the form of a check or stock. Mentally imagine yourself on that very moment of completing the transaction with joy. Feel it, harvest the emotion, and believe that an outcome or even better outcome is possible. Moreover, you should know, feel, and see in your minds eye what you will do when you become abundant in life's riches, how you will live, help others, and serve humanity.

The clearer the picture, the stronger the desire. If your desire is strong, your willingness to focus on the success and claiming it as yours will be made a seamless transaction. You must engage your heartfelt faith to secure a small step to success in each day. Stay engaged and keep moving toward your goals with gratitude and faith. After you have pictured your optimal vision and read your personal agreement to yourself, complete the meditative thought process with the words "and it is so, thank you for the blessing, thank you for expanding the quality of my life, and thank you for protecting me and my family." This will complete your exercise and you then send this petition into the world like a request that must be granted. You should be ready to receive what you want in any form or even a higher form or result. You need only use your willingness on yourself. You need not think of adversely harming others. You may then always use your self-will to force yourself to think about certain constructive things and doing certain beneficial actions. Every moment in doubt is a waste of time. Direct your attention to prosperity. The best thing you can do for the non-believers is to show them that you can achieve abundance and success. Your creative idea and plan *will* be a success if it is a strong desire that you are willing to go the distance to fulfill your dreams.

Do not tell the same old doubtful people of your plans and ideas. If you tell enough bitter people about your idea, their collective doubt or jealousy may weaken and sabotage your dreams. Surround yourself with experts in the field, people who are encouraging and insightful, people working toward a new outlook on life. Do not sink into the past by telling others about your difficulties or failures (unless in a secure peer-group where you have at least an unwritten contract of privacy and support). Interest yourself in becoming rich in life! Always try to see the positive side of your present state of affairs. Focus on optimistic conversation or beneficial events that have happened in your life. When you are willing, you must act the part. Do what you need to do. Make lists of things to do and begin doing them one by one. It may take a year to complete, but we must begin somewhere. Do each series of tasks and individual actions efficiently. Do them right the first time, and you need not fix it later. To do efficient and effective work, you need only to do one thing at a time and do not spread yourself too thin.

You need not try and mandate an outcome. The creative forces will unfold the correct and highest result for you. You merely need to organize your affairs so that you may receive the success and gladly accept the payoff. Overall, action is what will allow you to receive your abundance. Do only what can be done today, and tomorrow you can begin anew. In sum, put the faith, vision, and purpose behind your every action to accelerate your reaching higher abundance.

FIND OUT WHAT YOU REALLY WANT TO DO AND BE!

You should determine what you like or even what you love to do through this simple process. Write out a list of twenty things of interest to you. Continue adding and subtracting from the list. Over time, you will only have two or three things left because the supreme power will guide you toward your highest given talents. As a note, your purpose could be to study history or science, to read books, to write, to develop written content, to draw or create art and graphics, to travel, or to communicate with people. It should over time become more specific such as: I intend to become the best speaker or writer on the topic of politics or taxes, to complete a masters or doctorate in international business, to build the best Web site for information and links to success literature. It does not matter how you start, just begin the writing process! Just remember, a good talent (something you like to do and you are good at doing) combined with desire to become the best professional in this field will guarantee that you do and be what you love. At the least, you can become a teacher of your trade or profession and give back to the world by accelerating the learning of children or students in your field of love.

Without being boastful, you must convey the impression to others that you are advancing all that come in contact with you. Impress on others that you can add to their lives to promote your goals and ideals. Speak of your life and business as getting better and better all of the time. Act and feel as though you are very successful and that you are already rich in life and all of your needs are met. Incorporate a compassionate humility that you mix with poise, faith, confidence, and self-esteem. You need only speak when necessary, but your strong character and faithful confidence will attract the best people into your life.

If you are in a job and you cannot leave it to immediately follow your dreams, then do what you can in the evenings or weekends to hone your skills, plans, and education toward your goal. Use your present job skillfully to move in the direction that you want. There are thousands of people who have their business pay for their part-time education. Your contacts at work may lead to a better or different job. You must be prepared to discuss your dreams (what you want from life) in spoken words. You must know exactly what you want, and you must clarify and quantify it to others. You must be able to ask for and accept what you want out of life. You will need to interact with others who can help you.

This process of abundance, harmonization, and advancement will lead others to want to help you. Be ready for them and be open to forming alliances with them. Thus, your visions, meditations, and requests are traditionally answered by the universal power in the form of another person or entity being available to help and guide you. Be *ready* to tell them what you need, and do not be ashamed to ask for a win-win relationship with the people that come to you.

Remember, desires for prosperity are simply your spiritual movement toward a richer and fuller life. Prosperity and Abundance include: good health, quality relationships, good friends, a family of mutual respect, professional individual success, naturally expressing yourself and talents, and earning wealth. In conclusion, your quality of life is generally as good as your mind perceives is. Just when you think you are failing is the exact moment to continue your gratitude, meditation on you goals, and *action*! Just at that instant of doubt is when the highest good for you is ready to unfold. Even if the result is not exactly as you want, something better is very close and coming to you, and you have only been protected from a bad deal or relationship by waiting a little longer.

Tree of Life and The 9 Worlds

All living Nature is represented in the figure of the ancient Yggdrasill. The name historically means "Odin's Horse, chariot or seat." The living world is guided by the divinity which has its seat therein, as the Spirit in the body. The name in this sense fully coincides with the spirit of Old-Norse poetry: and the myth of the Yggdrassil appears throughout poetic allegory. The Tree or Worlds are really a symbol of the multidimensional structure of reality. *Image Below:

As you can see on the following page, the tree of life and its' worlds shows Consciousness & Awareness (SPIRIT) at top as a higher world and Hell at the bottom listed as unconsciousness and "living in illusion". There are several worlds or "states-of-being-ness" in-between which are indicative of our challenges and abilities to traverse through life effectively in our quest for freedom from illusion and misery. Overall, the key to the Yggdrassil is learning to properly use of the constructive metaphysical aspects the Yggdrassil to avoid a living in dis-harmony. Proper respect of the various worlds will allow the seeker to enter the flow of being and maintain power and ascension on the Tree. [xxxiv]

This also coincides somewhat with the tree of life of the Kaballah. As such, it is the using of these powers of mind, energy, balance, emotion, and action which bring the non-material into the material world. Cooperating with the unseen world to manifest your reality is also a piece of the philosophy that is focused on by researchers of the "Tree of Life" or Yggdrasil. It can also be discussed that there are 3 primary columns in the tree from left to right which symbolize the opposites of mildness and severity.

9 Metaphysical Worlds of the Yggdrasil – Copyright All Rights Reserved

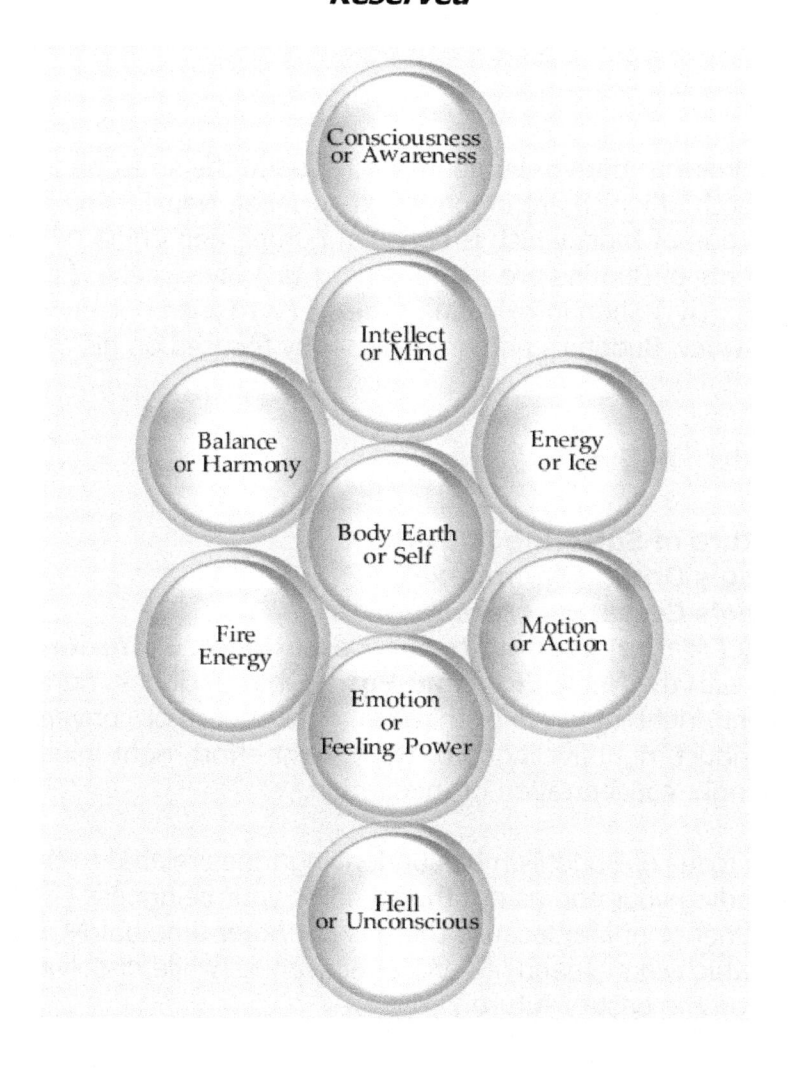

- Consciousness or Awareness
- Intellect or Mind
- Balance or Harmony
- Energy or Ice
- Body Earth or Self
- Fire Energy
- Motion or Action
- Emotion or Feeling Power
- Hell or Unconscious

This is a representation above of the metaphysical values/levels of the tree of life. Almost all cultures have some historical "Tree of Life". Note: the stele (carvings) of Ur-Nammu of Ur from 2100 BC is a depiction of the Tree of Life and Sun Moon God interaction. In the Nine Worlds of Norse Mythology, the 7 center worlds and be traversed, but the combination of the 7 can send either higher or below.

Buddhist Eight Fold Path to Happiness 四圣谛: - Indo-Aryan Thought

Budda: Siddhartha; born in Lumbini and raised in the small principality of Kapilvastu, both of which are in modern day Nepal. Nepal is the most Northern section of India which is between Europe and China. [xxxv] The five commandments of Buddha are : (i.) Kill not ; (ii.) Give freely ; (iii.) Bear no false witness ; (iv.) Shun intoxicating drinks ; (v.) Touch not thy neighbour's wife. Buddha's primary philosophy focused on his 4 Noble Truths.

4 Noble Truths 四圣谛:

1) **The Nature of Suffering (Dukkha):**
2) **Suffering's Origin (*Samudaya*)**
3) **Suffering's Cessation (*Nirodha*):**
4) **The Way (*Marga*) Leading to the Cessation of Suffering:** which provides us with the Noble **Eightfold Path**; which includes: right view or understanding, right intention or thinking, right speech or converse, right action or conduct, right livelihood or work, right effort, right mindfulness or awareness, right concentration or meditation.[xxxvi]

Much of the focus of Buddhism has underlying tones related to the issues of understanding your ego as not the same as your beingness (I AM-Ness), the impermanence of life because there is not other time but NOW, and awareness which can expand life and effectiveness while dissolving the ego's focus on the past or future..

Eightfold Path – The Rose-Croix Interpretation

1. Right View - This means to see, understand interpret, and believe the Highest Truth. It is simple to see things as misery and suffering. It is more noble to see life as a miracle and see beyond what the critical mind can see. The right view affords peace of mind, the ability to take action, and a sense of well-being. We eventually become what we think about all day; thus, our views and how we focus our attention are extremely important. Thinking bigger ideas of abundance, health, love, and so on, is a much greater force than negative ideas. Harmony leads to peace. Sometimes, the right view is simply to do what is in front of us, one thing at a time, and do it right the first time.

2. Right Intention - Intention is also similar to desire or purpose. If we are definite in our intentions and purpose, our dreams can unfold along the lines of our true path. Writing down our intentions is well enough, and has its effect, especially upon ourselves, in clarifying our vision and strengthening our faith; but it is not our oral or written petitions that get us what we want. In order to have abundance we do not need a "minute of prayer and concentration"; we need to "focus without ceasing during all hours." And by focus I mean holding steadily to your vision, with the purpose to cause idea creation into form. We can operate on a plane of mental harmony and good will, and we can flow constructively with life. It is better to not resist everything. We can allow life to unfold in conjunction with our constructive and faithful action. We can make the best of ourselves while in a state of well- being. Our highest truth is harmony, health, and success.

3. Right Speech - Guard and craft your speech carefully. Never speak of yourself, your affairs, or of anything else in a sympathy seeking or discouraging way. Never admit the possibility of failure, or speak in a way that implies disenchantment as a possibility. Never speak of life, career, or the economy as being hard, or of business conditions as being terrible. Times may be hard and business is bad for those who are operating in a Godless scramble within the competitive plane.   You are a constructive creator, your ideas help people, your ideas do not take away from anyone, you can create what you want, and you are above fear. When others are having hard times and poor business, you will find your greatest opportunities.

Right speech means the way you talk to others and to yourself. Train yourself to think and speak of life getting better and better with unlimited opportunities. Always speak in terms of advancement; to do otherwise is to deny your faith.

4. Right Action - Every act is, in itself, either effective or inefficient. Every inefficient act is a failure, and if you spend your life in doing inefficient acts, your whole life may become a loss. The more things you do, the worse for you, if all your acts are inefficient ones. On the other hand, if your every action is a success in itself, and if every act of your life is an efficient one, your whole life will be a success. The cause of failure is doing too many things in an inefficient manner without focus, and not doing enough things in an effective manner. You will see that it is a self-evident proposition that if you avoid inefficient acts, and if you do a sufficient number of efficient acts, you will harvest a richer and fuller life. Every action is either strong or weak; and when every one is strong, you are acting in the right way, which allows prosperity for you and your family. Every act can be made strong by holding your vision while you are doing it, and putting the whole power of your love, faith, gratitude, attention, and purpose into it. Further, our minds should facilitate ways and means to capture, receive, and harvest what life has to offer us so that we can use it for our betterment and to help others as well.

Never allow yourself to feel disappointed. You may expect to have a certain thing at a certain time, and not get it at that time; and this will appear as a loss. But if you hold to your faith, you will find that the failure is only apparent. Go on in the mindful way, and if you do not receive that thing, you will receive something so much better that you will see that the seeming loss was really a great success.

5. Right Livelihood - Right livelihood means that one should earn one's living in a Spiritual and joyous way. People should be able to follow their dreams and exercise their God-given talents in the form of livelihood and natural expression of their life force. Therefore, we should be able to feel work enjoyment while being rewarded for what we have given and produced for others. Right livelihood means creating win-win relationships and business dealings where everybody benefits while you use your divine gifts, talents, and labor. Your work is for the good of all involved and everyone receives some type of increase and advancement in their lives for interacting with you. Before you become fearful of success, realize that poverty and self-sacrifice are *not* pleasing to God. Furthermore, trying to play tricks with Karma will only lead to problems. And, remember that extreme altruism is no better and no nobler than extreme selfishness; both are mistakes. You need not entertain the thought of competition. You are to create, not to compete for what is already created.

You do not have to take anything away from any one. You do not have to cheat, obsessively bargain, or to take advantage in negotiations. You do not need to let any man work for you for less than he earns. You do not have to covet the property of others; no man has anything of which you cannot also achieve. You are to become a creator, not a competitor; you are going to get what you want, but in such a way that every other man will have more because of your actions.

6. Right Effort - Right effort can be seen as a prerequisite for the other principles of the path. Without effort, which is in itself an act of will, nothing can be achieved, whereas non-definite effort distracts the mind from its task, and confusion may be the consequence. Thus, you must really desire prosperous effort in your life. The more clear and definite you make your picture of your objectives, the stronger your desire will be; and the stronger your desire, the easier it will be to hold your mental energy fixed upon the picture of what you want. Behind your clear vision must be the purpose to realize it, to bring it out in tangible expression. Right efforts and work mixed with confident expectation or faith will be alive with results. And behind this purpose must be an invincible and unwavering belief that the thing is already yours and that you already have it in your mind. Thus, you need only to take possession of it mentally and receive it with open arms in-mind. Live in the new objective, mentally, until it takes form around you physically. No haste is required. However, we know effort is reduced by preparedness. Thus, being ready in your mind, body, and Spirit can enable seamless effort and flow of action. In the mental realm, enter at once into full enjoyment of the things you want. "Whatsoever things ye ask for when ye pray, believe that ye receive them, and ye shall have them," said The Great One.

7. Right Mindfulness - Right mindfulness is the controlled and perfected faculty of cognition. It is the mental ability to see things as they are, with clear consciousness. Usually, the cognitive process begins with an impression induced by perception, or by a thought, but then it does not stay with the mere impression. *A man's way of doing things is the direct result of the way he thinks about things.* To do things in a way you want to do them, you will have to acquire the ability to think the way you want to think; this is the first step toward achieving abundance. *To think what you want to think is to think the truth, regardless of appearances.*

Every man has the natural and inherent power to think what he wants to think, but it requires far more effort to do so than it does to think the thoughts that are suggested by surrounding appearances. To think according to the environment is easy; to think truth regardless of appearances is laborious and requires the expenditure of vast energy, mental power, love, and faith. This is possible for you if you are willing to train yourself and allow yourself to grow along these lines. The more you can harmoniously focus your mind while imagining all of your goal's delightful details, the better. This will bring the Universe in harmony with your highest good, which the Universe must answer for you. Mindfulness also implies that we should be aware that others on this earth are here to help us and may offer assistance. We should be in tune with these opportunities that may come from many places in the form of other people seeking us out.

8. Right Concentration - The eighth principle of the path, concentration, is described as one-pointed-ness of mind, meaning a state where all mental faculties are unified and directed onto one particular object. By thought, the thing you most sincerely desire is brought to you; by action you receive it. Hold concentration with faith and purpose. See the vision of yourself in the better environment. Act upon your present environment with all your heart, and with all your strength, and with all your concentration. Hold the vision of yourself with the right outcome or opportunity, with the purpose to get into it, and the faith that you will get into it, and are getting into it; but act in your present opportunity. Use your present situation or business as the means of getting a better one. Your vision of the right purpose or goal, if held with faith and purpose, will cause the Universe to move the right opportunity toward you; and your action, if performed in the light of harmonious intention and concentration, will cause you to move toward the opportunity. See the things you want as if they were actually around you all the time; see yourself as owning and using them.

Make use of them in imagination just as you will use them when they are your tangible possessions. Dwell upon your mental picture until it is clear and distinct, and then take the mental attitude of ownership toward everything in that picture. Take possession of it, in mind, in the full faith that it is actually yours. Hold to this mental ownership; do not waiver for an instant in the faith that it is real. And remember this about gratitude; be thankful for your life and desires "at all times" as you expect to be when it has taken form. The man who can sincerely thank the Universe for the things he owns only in imagination, has real faith. He will have abundance and peace; he will cause the creation of whatsoever he wants.

The present moment is the essence of your "being-ness" Your awareness can also be interpreted as your "Life Force Consciousness". Thus, existing in the moment while in harmony with the universe can be construed as "Peace of Mind". Remaining contemplative in action is also part of being in the moment.

Summary of The Eightfold Path

Becoming a warrior at true peace with yourself is the key. Bridging your actions to your Spiritual mind and body is where focus, poise, effectiveness, and success emerge. To advance quickly, man must form a clear and definite mental image of the things he wishes to have, to do, or to become; and he must hold this mental image in his thoughts while being deeply grateful to the Universe that all his highest needs and desires are granted to him. The man who wishes to have an abundant and prosperous life must spend his leisure hours in contemplating his vision, and in earnest thanksgiving that the reality is being given to him. Too much stress cannot be laid on the importance of frequent contemplation of the mental image, coupled with unwavering faith and devout gratitude. This is the process by which the impression is given to the Universe, and the creative forces are set in motion. Your mind will then begin working with you to allow right attention, concentration, and livelihood on a level of love, harmony, faith, and gratitude. Defining your purpose in life or aiming towards specific outcomes while allowing them to unfold in higher and better ways will be where the Spiritual miracles appear. Moreover, allowing your talents, true place, and right career to become part of your life will also be part of your journey. Ultimately, intertwining your concentration, mind, speech, and view to your action will be the missing link of success. Combining the sharpened mind with action is where your daily results begin to add up and build momentum towards growth and expansion.[xxxvii]

*Passages compiled from several authors with insights from Prof. Incognito and W. D. Wattles included.

Creative Success Executive Summary

1. We are all connected to the Source of Creation, the Universal Spirit, The Life Force, and Nature Itself. We are all created of source, but because of our individual consciousness, we each have our own "I AM" or "Being-ness" in concert with the Universe.
2. Our thinking and the focused power of our thought can accelerate or change the direction of the universal forces that apply to us. We are divinely inspired with creative feelings. However, the focus of our habitual thinking and feelings draws energy and manifestations from the universe.
3. Our Views and Thinking are always present. Learning how to constructively use our thinking is the key. Control, discipline, concentration and focus are skills of mastery that can vastly augment our abilities to be creators.
4. Learning to think about what we want to Experience is Vital to draw closer to Natural Expression and our individual Life Force. We do have the ability to control our thoughts. Most of us have never tried controlled thinking or directed thought.
5. If we are determined to become "self-reliant", the universe will recognize this decision of Response-Ability and begin to cooperate with us and help us.
6. We must also befriend the world and embrace it. When we begin to cooperate with Supreme Intelligence, we begin to flow with the currents of the world and it desires to help us. This mental action toward a harmonious, loving and peaceful relationship with the SOURCE, will allow us to REQUEST, ASK, RECEIVE, and MANIFEST much more easily.

7. Prosperity comes in many forms such as: Health, Ideas, Creativity, Right Work, Love, Relationships, Natural Expression of our Talents and even Economic Success.
8. Developing a consciousness of BEING WORTHY OF PROSPERITY is critically important. We must believe that the world wants to lavish us with creativity, happiness, health, the strength and knowledge to serve others and humanity, and true abundance
9. For any prosperity that we have ever received, we can practice giving sincere thanks for our gifts and FEEL the supply and abundance. Our outpouring of thanks and gratitude can open the portals of the universe to shower health, love, peace, and wealth upon you and yours.
10. Affirming our good and our connection to Spirit can also create worthiness and a thankful heart. Tune in with the LIFE FORCE of ALL. Use the spoken word to declare what you want from
11. Spirit is LOVE, PEACE and HARMONY. When you think from a perspective of love, peace and harmony while making requests TO the SUPREME, your requests will be "Tens-of-Times" more powerful than any other base thought of negative tendency. "Make known your requests with Thanksgiving." Bless and praise your body, your health, your world, your successes, and your gifts and the WORLD will begin to bless and praise YOU as an EXTENSION of IT.
12. We must learn to graduate from hope to belief. From wishing to the certainty of Faith and transform our mindset toward of state of confident knowing.
13. We must obtain the habit of REALIZATION of the Divine Presence. This UNITY is many times more powerful that any sense of Separateness.
14. With Unity with or toward the Supreme, our clarity and awareness become greater. With Gratitude and Harmony, our alertness and curiosity become more profound. With awareness and inquisitiveness, we are more inundated with ideas, creative thoughts, and greater dreams of growth.

15. The powers of Attraction have several vital points. Reinventing yourself and your personal attributes is different from the concept of wanting a tangible thing. As for attracting and changing our character, we can change mentally each day toward an ideal or

objective. As an example, if we want to become an expert in a specific field such as "Sports or Teaching", we think of these things, feed ourselves with the ideas related to these fields, act the part, learn the part, and BE THE PART. We ACT "AS IF" we ARE what we desire. You see, to become, we must internalize in mind and heart that which we seek as well as mastering the external knowledge, experiences and facets of the art.

16. With the manifestation of objects, we should learn to use the same process. However with things, you simply don't see yourself as being something new and enhanced, but you are seeing yourself in possession of something that your have declared, specified, mentally pictured, and visualized. With both, we are taught that it is vitally important to emotionalize the mental pictures with an earnest and sincere belief of possession and having comingled with emotions such as joy, worthiness, appreciation, and thanks.

17. It is sort of like enjoying the past. The past happened, but it can seem like a dream. Thus, <u>if we can pre-dream with sincerity and positive emotion</u>, then our manifestations of the future are pushed into the universal field of the formless and begin to coalesce toward taking formation.

18. "We are all in Mind and what we think earnestly into-it is taken up and done unto us. This means that as we think with heartfelt, constructive-faith, it will be done. We cannot think one way one day and change our thought the next and hope to get the desired results. We must be very clear in our thought, sending out only such thoughts as we wish to see manifested in our condition."

19. We are conceiving sense impressions all day. Sometimes are conceptions are great and wonderful ideas. When an idea has such presence and is thought consuming, we can take are hard look at the thought and determine if this new idea requires our boldness of thought, analysis, and action. If it does, be can begin to "Think-into-it" We can conceive it, better comprehend it, affirm it, and begin to know it mentally.

20. The Truth of It will either begin to appear quickly or we can let it go. If it becomes a burning desire, we will begin to earnestly feel the certain possibility of the idea, health, abundance or prosperity.

21. Remember to embody and feel consciously what you want and desire. Become it, Be it. Enjoy the thoughts and expectations of creation and transformation.
22. Do not focus on Toxic People, Rage Addicts, The Struggle and Hope Addicts, The Negaholics, The Jealous and Hateful, The Self Proclaimed Deprived, or Global Scarcity. You would not expose yourself to a deadly toxin or germ if you could avoid it. Thus, you must be a prudent steward of your mind, spirit and body.
23. If possible, avoid feeding yourself with depressing TV, WEB, or Radio news that are simply focused upon Destruction based Entertainment. This type of news can be a waste of time, a huge distraction, and affect your psyche. What you continually over-feed yourself, you become. If this is your primary visual and audio input, you may become a very confused or disoriented person.
24. Focus your mind on becoming your best and moving toward your highest expression of life. Learn to be your best!
25. If you have trouble imagining the best, find someone you admire and begin to copy: their character, path, education, habits, and success. Surround yourself those who believe in the inherent goodness of people and the world.

26. Encircle yourself with those who are already RICH IN LIFE, FULL OF SPIRIT, and EAGER FOR KNOWLEDGE.
27. Associate with those who are pulling for you, supportive of your dreams, and those who believe in your potential. Bless and support their dreams in RETURN.
28. Don't' say things that decree against the Good Will of the Universal Mind.
29. Learn to refute hate, anger, poverty and other ills. They are none of your concern. Become all you can and work to improve your health, mind and prosperity. THEN, you can help all those you choose with your Secrets.
30. All is Right with Your world. Because you are centered in gratitude, harmony, action and good will. Because you are Strong and working to maintain your balance, YOU ARE EVER INCREASING and GROWING in PROSPERITY.
31. From selfish motives alone, if from no loftier reason, we cannot afford to find fault or to hate or even to hold in mind anything

against any living soul. The God who is love cannot hear the prayer of the man who is not love. Love and co-operation will yet be found to be the greatest business principle on earth. "God is Love."

32. Seek to find what is wrong with the WORLD, and this will be shown to you. This Wrongness will justify your claims about realism. You may then become righteous about the defects of humanity. You may become obsessed with blame, victimhood and anger. If it becomes all consuming, you may even become sick or have a breakdown. THUS, FIND WHAT IS RIGHT WITH THE WORLD, and focus on what is good. With this new found focus and concentration, your confidence and strength can be built much more easily while your attention and focus will be more laser focused.

33. However, if you Look for what is RIGHT with the world, YOU WILL CONTINUE TO FIND IT WITH EASE. Finding things to be grateful for will allow you to develop a "Thankful Heart". Faith and Knowingness becomes relatively easy with a Thankful Heart.

EXERCISES AND PRACTICE

Exercise #1: A good practice is to sit and realize that you are a center of Divine attraction, that all things are coming to you, that the power within is going out and drawing back all that you will ever need. Don't argue about it, just do it, and when you have finished leave it all to the Law, knowing that it will be done. Declare that all life, all love and power are now in your life. Declare that you are now in the midst of plenty. Stick to it even though you may not as yet see the result. It will work and those who believe the most always get the most. Think of the Law as your friend while always looking out for your interest. Trust completely in it and it will bring your good to you.

Exercise #2: A good practice for the enlargement of thought is daily to see ourselves in a little bigger place, filled with more of activity, surrounded with increased influence and power; feel more and more that things are coming to us; see that much more is just ahead, and so far as possible, know that we now have all that we see and all that we feel. Affirm that you are that larger thing; that you are now entered into that larger life; feel that something within is drawing more to you; live with the idea and let the concept grow, expecting only the biggest and the best to happen. Never let small thoughts come into your mind, and you will soon find that a larger and greater experience has come into your life.

Exercise #3: Daily practice the truth and daily die to all error-thought. Spend more time receiving and realizing the, presence of the Most High and less time worrying. Wonderful power will come to the one who believes and trusts in that Power in which he has come to believe. Know that all good and all God is with you; All Life and All Power; and never again say, "I fear," but always, "I trust, because 'I know in whom I have believed.'" Speak in this inner silence and say, "I am one with the Almighty; I am one with all life, with all power, with all presence. I AM, I AM, I AM." Listen to the silence. From out of the seeming void the voice of peace will answer the waiting soul, "All is well."

Exercise #4: Before you take Action: First, you must be quiet within yourself. You must not be confused by any outward appearance. Never become disturbed by effects. They didn't make themselves and have no intelligence to contradict you. Be quiet until you realize the presence of absolute Intelligence all around you, of the Mind that knows. Now get a perfect picture of just what you desire. You cannot get a picture unless you know what it is you want. Put your mind in touch with Universal Mind, saying just what you are waiting for. Ask for it, believe that you are receiving it, and wait. After a few minutes declare that you now know, even though you may not seem to know, yet in the depths of consciousness you have received the impression. Give thanks that you now receive. Do this every day until you get some direction. It is sometimes a good thing to do this just before going to sleep. Never, after you have done this, deny the knowledge that has been given you. The time will come when some idea will begin to take form. Wait for it and, when it does appear, act upon it with all the conviction of one who is perfectly sure of himself. You have gotten understanding straight from the source of all understanding, knowledge from the source of knowledge. All can do this if they will be persistent. It is a sure direction and guidance and will never fail us. But we must be sure that we are not denying in other moments what we affirm in the moments of Faith. In this way we will make fewer mistakes and in time our lives will be controlled by supreme wisdom and understanding. [xxxviii]

More Metaphysical Issues & Insights

Harmonious Relationships: Connected with all there is that is good, harvesting and having a harmonious relationship with the world through various philosophical exercises, using gratitude for any of your gifts on a daily basis can grow your expectation of good and faith. It is much easier to be connected when you have set aside or removed destructive thinking such as resentments, jealously or the seven deadly sins.

Desires: Desires are good and excellent. Desires can focus you on enriching your life and following your true direction. Cultivating desires into reality is vital for change, innovation, and improvement. You would not have a desire unless it was possible, but select desires where you have a solid sphere of possibility. An earnest and heartfelt desire is what allows us to seize upon opportunities and develop plans.

Plans: A plan or objective is fundamental in the clarification and specificity of your desire. A large majority of people are afraid to specify what they intend to do. Transcending this fear and taking bold action upon your plans and strategies allows for the growth and manifestation of your idea into a reality

Vision A vision is important in that you clarify the path to your short-term and long-term enrichment of yourself, your goals, teamwork, or relationships.

Mission: A mission is important in that you can quantify and clarify a path to an outcome or ending strategy.

Having, Emotion, and Feelings: Mentally understanding the outcome or result as if you have it already is very important. It also allows you to qualify the consequences. It further provides you with feelings surrounding the outcome. Harvesting positive feelings surrounding the outcome is very important to energize a desire, mission, visualization, and result.

Visualization, Pictures, Imagination, Sending It Out

Mental visualization of your objectives holds great importance in the clarity of what you intend to do along the way and what you desire as an end result. Seeing what you intend to do and what you desire and plan as if it is real is a complex mental exercise, but vital to the codification and building of the objective so as to assist the manifestation of the result. Seeing *exactly* what you desire and intend causes you to specify your wants and desires. The stronger and longer you can hold your ideal in your mind's eye, the better.

Attention Focus: Pointing your mental faculties toward the individual actions required to achieve a task, project, or goal is what causes effectiveness, as long as your acts are efficient. Continuous and persistent thinking and action toward your work, goal, project, or desired outcome can funnel or intensify the energy in a specific direction.

Efficiently and Effectively: Completion and closure of acts and tasks one-by-one in a successful manner is what creates momentum toward an objective with no need to go backward.

Presence, Awareness, Doing: Thinking and planning are most crucial. However, boldness and action are what may cause events to happen and people to be attracted to you. Therefore, contemplation mixed with action is the optimal, blended solution.

Cause/Effect: "Like Attracts Like": Every action has a reaction. Types of actions and thoughts attract similar actions and thoughts. Kindness tends to bring kindness. Respect tends to bring respect. Additionally, constructive thinking tends to bring constructive opportunities and events to the individual.

Increase: All mankind tends to be attracted to those who can bring them more life or enrichment. If an individual projects life and opportunity, then he or she will attract similar minds.

Insight and Restraint: Insight and restraint contain the ability to think something over, discuss it with others, or seek out counsel from others who understand or know the subject well without acting hastily. Thus, the opinion of experts and consequences are a valid consideration in thinking and acting.

Love, Forgiveness, Harmony, Dissipating Discouragement: Cultivating love and forgiveness can dispel otherwise destructive thoughts. Great minds can look back on things they love or loved, and re-harness that emotion.

Minding Your Own Business: There is something very real in taking care of yourself and your affairs. As such, your enhanced mind, body, soul, and financial affairs allow you to help those whom you love and serve humanity in better ways. The best way to be of service to humanity and your loved ones is to make the best of yourself.

Gratitude, Enthusiasm, Faith: A sincere heartfelt gratitude for life and its gifts will allow the flow of good to you. Systematic recognition of people or things to be thankful for along with gratitude may facilitate an expectation of good and growth of inherent faith. Integrating this confident expectation with your aspirations creates great power.

Guarded Speech, Response/Ability: Speaking of only positive things can attract opportunity and friends. Keeping your desires and goals close to you will keep them from becoming dissipated energy. Sharing your desires and goals with those who support, encourage, and assist you can be a positive exercise and help harvest constructive feedback.

Change/Insanity: Not evolving while continuing to do things that are failures or destructive actions tends to prevent any growth.

Creating Versus Competing: It seems that many people feel that competition causes a limited supply. However, from a supply or abundance standpoint, individuals can create without competing, to serve humanity. As an example, an individual who creates a new cure to solve a common health problem is not competing against the world, but helping it.

Right Livelihood and Labor of Love: Having a labor of love can cause effectiveness and efficiency through energetic work. Doing something that you believe in or selling a product that you have faith in, can make your job much easier or even fun. Having fun with work is a divine right.

Blessing, Praise, Protection, and Expansion: Persons who engage in a metaphysical approach seem to enjoy a greater state of well-being and success when they bless their relationship with the Universe, bless their loved ones, bless their home, and give thanks for their health on a daily basis.

Gratitude, Religion and Great Thinkers:

If the only prayer you say in your life is "Thank you," that would suffice. -- **Meister Eckhart**

Roman Empire: Take full account of the excellencies which you possess, and in gratitude remember how you would hanker after them, if you had them not. --**Marcus Aurelius**

Judaism: In the Jewish faith, gratitude is a critical component of worship. In the Hebrew Scriptures, the Psalms are saturated with thanksgiving to God: "O Lord my God, I will give thanks to you forever" (30:12), and "I will give thanks to the Lord with my whole heart "(9:1).

Christianity: In the Christian faith, Philippians IV sums up the Christian attitude toward gratitude. See Below:

Philippians IV

4 Rejoice in the Lord always. Again I will say, rejoice! 5 Let your gentleness be known to all men. The Lord [is] at hand. 6 Be anxious for nothing, but in everything by prayer and supplication, with thanksgiving, let your requests be made known to God; 7 and the peace of God, which surpasses all understanding, will guard your hearts and minds through Christ Jesus. 8 Finally, brethren, whatever things are true, whatever things [are] noble, whatever things [are] just, whatever things [are] pure, whatever things [are] lovely, whatever things [are] of good report, if [there is] any virtue and if [there is] anything praiseworthy -- meditate on these things. 9 The things which you learned and received and heard and saw in me, these do, and the God of peace will be with you. 10 But I rejoiced in the Lord greatly that now at last your care for me has flourished again; though you surely did care, but you lacked opportunity. 11 Not that I speak in regard to need, for I have learned in whatever state I am, to be content: 12 I know how to be abased, and I know how to abound. Everywhere and in all things I have learned both to be full and to be hungry, both to abound and to suffer need. 13 I can do all things through Christ who strengthens me.

Read the above statements and passages from the Old Scriptures and other quotes and think about: gentleness, thanksgiving, constructive petitions, request for blessings, a sincere feeling of gratitude, meditating on noble and optimistic thoughts, rejoicing in life, and even blessing yourself and your future.

Unfolding Detachment Protected for Higher Good: When we become too attached or dependent on an external person, place, thing, or result, we can become disappointed with other people and things. It is good to expect the best, but it is also smart to allow for something better to unfold. Thus, trying to control a specific outcome without any flexibility can inhibit the Universe from its creativity.

Receiving, Valuing, Deserving: Many people from around the world feel unworthy of abundance. Many people do not value themselves, their service, their talents, and work. It is very important to learn to feel worthy, unique, and deserving of good. Moreover, you should become mentally open to receiving all good in life. Further, people should be careful to create ways to receive the good into their lives from the Universe and from others. Example: Accepting a compliment from another person.

Other People and They Are Sent to Help You: When you engage a mentality of abundance and harmonious Spiritual thinking, your mind will expand and increase while radiating love, abundance, and health. Thus, your powers of attraction will increase. The Universe will send people to help you. It will be your job to select and allow them to assist you in a win-win relationship to expand your abundance where all can achieve a richer and fuller life through these ventures.

Resistance and Flow: Types of resistance that inhibit your abundance, health, and connection with Spirit are: resentment, jealousy, anger, judgment, criticism, hatred, greed, pride, and mental laziness. Other subtle resistance is to institutions, conformity, and adapting. It is better to adapt than to perish, while maintaining your unique qualities

Willingness: Willingness is the key to advancement. Be willing to take action, take a chance, or risk failure or embarrassment. Without willingness, you may never engage mental, Spiritual, or physical action that leads to good. Willingness is a vital ingredient toward successful visualization, belief, action, planning, and success. Am I willing to believe, to try, to engage? Can it be done? And why not?

Hoarding and Change: Holding onto old counterproductive ideas & un-needed things can keep you from growth, Spiritual flow, and expansion. Taking an inventory of mental ideas and material things must be done. Eliminating the ideas, things, people, and actions that create inconvenience, frustration, clutter, and resentment will allow freedom and harmony in your life.

Recognition of Cause: It can be a fundamental mistake if you give yourself too much credit for anything good that you receive from life. Additionally, it can be a disastrous mistake to continue to blame God and the Universe for anything bad that you receive from life.

Sanity, Root Out Cause, Unlimited Potential: Root out the cause of your failures, your inconveniences, your frustration, and your mental or Spiritual disabilities. If you have a problem, there may be a cause. If you injured yourself engaging in a specific activity, you may avoid this activity in the future or better prepare for it next time. Otherwise, you may pay for this repeated action in the form of more pain and suffering. If you have a relationship that always seems to leave you in pain, then you may need to avoid this person if you are spiritually whole and the other person is not.

Giving Without Expectation, Tithing : Taking time to give money, service, or goods to divine recipients will create an untold flow in your life. Life requires circulation of your ideas, your things, and your service to humanity. With this giving, it is virtually guaranteed that your life will be blessed and protected through your giving of yourself. You are not doing this to take advantage of the law. You do this to expand your Spiritual existence, keep the flow, and give back. Expecting something in return is not needed because the Universe will provide opportunity for you by your embracing this process.

Good Deeds Action & Karma: You may feel you have wronged many people. You may even feel guilty for past deeds or encounters. However, if you feel remorse and intend to act as a better person for now on, then you have made progress. In any event, your day-to-day action and character of goodness and kindness will build your positive energy where the world has decided to protect you and serve you.

Meek Defined: Open Mind, Faith in Universe, Will of God, Spirit Before Ego: Meek is not weak. It is strong, confident, cooperative, and advantageous. Developing an honest appraisal of yourself can be healthy. You can always improve yourself, your credentials, your relationships and your business. Putting your ego first can be dangerous. When somebody has hurt your feelings, said you are wrong, said "no" to you, or otherwise attacked you, it is best to analyze (when possible) and discuss the issue with another supportive person before retaliating with e-mail, phone, letter, or in person.

Peace and Serenity Are Needed for Concentration: Peace allows growth. Clarity and concentration are primary keys to serenity. Being able to operate on a plane with singleness of mind can allow you to achieve great things. A person who cannot focus and achieve one thing at a time may never cross "the finish line" with any dream, goal, or aspiration. Overall, if you allow resentment, frustration, hate of another, or fear to dominate your thoughts, then your effectiveness will be diminished. Hard work is required to keep you focused and concentrating on bettering yourself. Overall, your freedom, vitality and wholeness depend on your effectiveness.

Visualizing Completed Transaction With Joy: We have mentioned visualization. Do not forget that you should visualize things and plans as you would have them. You should believe that they are yours in mind. Paint your ideal outcome on the mental screen in your mind's eye. Believe that it is completed. Fuse your image with love and gratitude. Celebrate its reception in your mind. Believe that you have the proper channels to receive what is coming to you. Send your vision and petition into the Universe and repeat the exercise for fantastic results.

Treasure Map and Wheel of Fortune: If you cannot paint the mental picture as clearly as you would want, then try to use the material world to enhance your mind. Cut out pictures of the ideal things you want. Put them into a collage or on poster board. Rip out images of the home you desire, people having fun, distant places that you want to visit, or the lifestyle and types of relationships that you desire. This action can help you amalgamate the images to imprint them on your subconscious mind. View them daily and place them in a prominent place. Overall, imagine having these things in your quite time. Sense the joy of receiving all of it full

Balance

Enough stress can not be laid on balance between body, mind and spirit. Sounds easy, but all people need to honor their bodies, improve their minds, and evolve their spiritual nature. Many organizations emphasize that when you are "out of balance", you have placed too much energy and focus in only one area of your life. Example: You can work to hard or exercise too much and actually hurt your immune system or a muscle etc.

Joy/Happiness

Feeling good is subjective and also relative. Some mystic organizations believe that feeling bad is a byproduct of your actions, thinking or omissions.

Atonement and At-One-Ment

Many organizations from the ancient churches to mystical organizations encourage self analysis, confession, amends, atonement and even retribution. This spiritual house cleaning can free the mind from guilt, shame or even self defeating thoughts. Forgiveness of others and self is highly important for most philosophies and religions.

Peace of Mind

Peace of Mind transcends all material desires. Most philosophers from Socrates to Kant up to present times define happiness as "Peace of Mind" As we know, each of us has our own subjective version of what peace of mind would be; however, this peace would of course imply faith and a freedom from pain, ignorance, worry, mental misery, and self destructive thoughts.

Wealth and Opulence

Wealth and Opulence are keenly tied to worthiness. Sometimes our minds are too wrapped up in hoarding and not circulating our abundance. Thus, it is sometimes good to simply act "AS IF" you were rich and "PLAY THE PART". Other times, it is best to treat yourself to something that you deserve such as a vacation, new car, massage, hobby enhancement, clothes, ideal home, tools for effective work, or other. When you begin to treat yourself on a higher level, your body responds and the world also responds.

Affirmations and Meditations silence.

It can be argued that many people are best served by learning to become silent and open to the universe. After research, it is clear that there are 2 types of personalities. One personality is best served with quiet communion with their higher self. The other is best served with affirmations and prayers that assist in changing their thought. As you can see, one is active and the other is inactive or slowing down. A combination of both would be excellent, and many people focus on one system at a time.

Open Willing Change

Life is Growth. Life is also a series of changes. Being prepared for change by always growing is key to peaceful transition. We should keep seeking life and spirit and not become too comfortable in the same position.

Desire Specific and Purpose

Specific dreams and desires are good. Most people are simply too timid to define what they want from life.

Natural Expression

When you reach periods in your life that you are truly happy, it is probably because you are expressing yourself naturally on a level of spirit, relationships, creation, and livelihood.

Character Development

The development of character means pruning off the old branches that "simply have not worked for you". These branches could be lifestyle choices that do not work, jobs that do not work, relationships that do not work, or even your thinking and preconceptions that have failed.

Boldness Action Comfort

Getting out of your comfort zone and taking some small action in the direction of your needs, wants or desires can sometimes be the utter spark of creation. This can sometimes create a whirlwind of activities, insights, ideas, help from others and so on.

Life & Abundance is Everywhere

The world is overflowing with supply. The birds and animals of the world want not. There is a never-ending quantity of material and substance to create what is needed on this earth and plane. If something ever becomes scarce, a more efficient substitute is prepared or invented. Ideas, creativity and imagination have solved millions of challenges in just our lifetime alone.

Separateness

If you feel like you simply don't fit, or that you are not part of the world, it could be that you have lost your connectedness to the universal force and spirit. If by some luck, you don't believe in a supreme being, then simply express gratitude to your food, your ancestors, your body, for your abilities, your home, etc. This action of thankfulness to ALL will bring you into a relationship to the ALL. English speaking peoples call it GOD. The Ancient Taoists and Buddhists called it by its name TAO or DAO 道 meaning the path or the "way". Tao can be roughly stated to be the flow of the universe, or the force behind the natural order.

Harmony Gratitude

Feeling Gratitude and Focusing upon any thoughts of Thankfulness will invariably change your thinking and how you react to life. It will also charge your spirit with the expectation of faith and opportunity.

The mathematical proof of Gratitude and Success is below:

G= Gratitude, Thankfulness, Praise
F= Feeling Gratitude or Love Energy - Thinking it.
C= Constructive Action
N = Negative Thought or Toxic Exposure to Low Energy Forces
S = Probabilities of Success and Peace.

Equation: $(G \times F)(C) - N = S$ (Success & Peace)

Axiom: *It is far easier to have a living faith with heartfelt gratitude.*

You are chosen, naturally unique, knowing

What ever your race, believe that it is good and great. Whatever your education, believe that you can be better as more knowledge and understanding of the laws of life are needed. Regardless of your appearances, you can look better, improve yourself, be healthy, and enhance your image in your unique way. It does not matter what religion or philosophy you adhere to, your spiritual knowledge and awareness can be cultivated to a new dimension where peace of mind is yours. You are a Genius. You have been chosen to do great things and live a significant life. You have talent from the universe. You must allow your assets and skills to be honed and sharpened. Do not die with your vision and talents unused. You are special, and you can be whatever you want within your sphere of availability and grow accordingly toward your destiny. There is nothing wrong with being confident in who you are. Only good can come from growth. Sometimes change is difficult, but the re-invention or rebirth of your true self is available NOW. [xxxix]

Initiation of Mastery Exercises in 28 Parts

Introduction: Nature compels us all to move through life. We could not remain stationary however much we wished. Every right-thinking person wants not merely to move through life like a sound-producing, perambulating plant, but to develop - to improve - and to continue the development mentally to the close of physical life.

Some men seem to attract success, power, wealth, attainment, with very little conscious effort; others conquer with great difficulty; still others fail altogether to reach their ambitions, desires and ideals. Why is this so? Why should some men realize their ambitions easily, others with difficulty, and still others not at all?

1. The attitude of mind necessarily depends upon what we think. Therefore, the secret of all power, all achievement and all possession depends upon our method of thinking. The world without is a reflection of the world within. Harmony in the world within means the ability to control our thoughts, and to determine for ourselves how any experience is to affect us.

2. Our difficulties are largely due to confused ideas and ignorance of our true interests. Thought is energy. Active thought is active energy; concentrated thought is a concentrated energy. Thought concentrated on a definite purpose becomes power. This is the power which is being used by those who do not believe in the virtue of poverty, or the beauty of self-denial. They perceive that this is the talk of weaklings. The value of the subconscious is enormous; it inspires us; it warns us; it furnishes us with names, facts and scenes from the storehouse of memory. It directs our thoughts, tastes, and accomplishes tasks so intricate that no conscious mind, even if it had the power, has the capacity for. On the spiritual side, it is the source of ideals, of aspiration, of the imagination, and is the channel through which we recognize our Divine Source, and in proportion as we recognize this divinity do we come into an understanding of the source of power.

3. It is our attitude of mind toward life which determines the experiences with which we are to meet; if we expect nothing, we shall have nothing; if we demand much, we shall receive the greater portion. The world is harsh only as we fail to assert ourselves. The criticism of the world is bitter only to those who cannot compel room for their ideas. It is fear of this criticism that causes many ideas to fail to see the light of day.

Exercise: I want you to not only be perfectly still, and inhibit all thought as far as possible, but relax, let go, let the muscles take their normal condition; this will remove all pressure from the nerves, and eliminate that tension which so frequently produces physical exhaustion.

4. The greatest and most marvelous power which this "I" has been given is the power to think, but few people know how to think constructively, or correctly, consequently they achieve only indifferent results. Most people allow their thoughts to dwell on selfish purposes, the inevitable result of an infantile mind. When a mind becomes mature, it understands that the germ of defeat is in every selfish thought.

One of the strongest affirmations which you can use for the purpose of strengthening the will and realizing your power to accomplish, is, "I can be what I will to be." Every time you repeat it realize who and what this "I" is; try to come into a thorough understanding of the true nature of the "I"; if you do, you will become invincible; that is, provided that your objects and purposes are constructive and are therefore in harmony with the creative principle of the Universe.

5. In the domain of mind and spirit, in the domain of practical power, such an estate is yours. You are the heir! You can assert your heirship and possess, and use this rich inheritance. Power over circumstances is one of its fruits, and health, harmony and prosperity are assets upon its balance sheet. It offers you poise and peace. It costs you only the labor of studying and harvesting its great resources. It demands no sacrifice, except the loss of your limitations, your servitudes, your weakness. It clothes you with self-honor, and puts a scepter in your hands. To gain this estate, three processes are necessary: You must earnestly desire it. You must assert your claim. You must take possession.

Exercise: Now, go to your room, enter your relaxed state, and mentally select a place which has pleasant associations. Make a complete mental picture of it, see the buildings, the grounds, the trees, friends, associations, everything complete. At first, you will find yourself thinking of everything under the sun, except the ideal upon which you desire to concentrate. But do not let that discourage you. Persistence will win, but persistence requires that you practice these exercises every day without fail.

6. To be in tune with eternal truth we must possess poise and harmony within. In order to receive intelligence the receiver must be in tune with the transmitter. Every thought sets the brain cells in action; at first the

substance upon which the thought is directed fails to respond, but if the thought is sufficiently refined and concentrated, the substance finally yields and expresses perfectly. Finding harmony with the universal power will bring you great power and resources.

7. Visualization is the process of making mental images, and the image is the mold or model which will serve as a pattern from which your future will emerge. Make the image clear and clean-cut, hold it firmly in the mind and you will gradually and constantly bring the thing nearer to you. You can be what "you will to be." You should see the end before a single step is taken; so you are to picture in your mind what you want; you are sowing the seed, but before sowing any seed you want to know what the harvest is to be.

This is Idealization. If you are not sure, return to the quiet meditation or prayer daily until the picture becomes plain. Make the Mental Image; make it clear, distinct, perfect; hold it firmly; the ways and means will develop; supply will follow the demand; you will be led to do the right thing at the right time and in the right way. Earnest Desire will bring about Confident Expectation, and this in turn must be reinforced by Firm Demand.

Exercise: Visualize a friend, see your friend exactly as you last saw him, see the room, the furniture, recall the conversation, now see his face, see it distinctly, now talk to him about some subject of mutual interest; see his expression change, watch him smile. Can you do this? OR Take a pack of matches and pour them all out on a table top. Mix them up and then place them back in the box one by one making each of the tips point in the same direction. An excellent and easy visualization mastery exercise.

8. As the one purpose of life is growth, all principles underlying existence must contribute to give it effect. Thought, therefore, takes form and the law of growth eventually brings it into manifestation. You may freely choose what you think, but the result of your thought is governed by an immutable law. Any line of thought persisted in cannot fail to produce its result in the character, health and circumstances of the individual.

The law of attraction will certainly and unerringly bring to you the conditions, environment, and experiences in life, corresponding with your habitual, characteristic, predominant mental attitude. Not what you think once in a while when you are in church, or have just read in a good book, BUT your predominant mental attitude is what counts.

Combining harmonious thought and visualization with the great powers within is where true energy and creation comes from. Place yourself in position to receive this power. As it is Omnipresent, it must be within you. We know that this is so because we know that all power is from within, but it must be developed, unfolded, & cultivated; in order to do this we must be receptive and open.

9. Hold in mind the condition desired; affirm it as an already existing fact. This indicates the value of a powerful affirmation. By constant repetition it becomes a part of ourselves. We are actually changing ourselves; are making ourselves what we want to be.

To think correctly, accurately, we must know the "Truth." We must realize that truth is the vital principle of the Universal Mind and is Omnipresent. For instance, if you require health, a realization of the fact that the "I" in you is spiritual and that all spirit is one; that wherever a part is the whole must be, will bring about a condition of health, because every cell in the body must manifest the truth as you see it.

If you require Love try to realize that the only way to get love is by giving it, that the more you give the more you will get, and the only way in which you can give it, is to fill yourself with it, until you become a magnet.

If you require Wealth a realization of the fact that the "I" in you is one with the Universal mind which is all substance, and is Omnipotent, will assist you in bringing into operation the law of attraction which will bring you into vibration with those forces which make for success and bring about conditions of power and affluence in direct proportion with the character and purpose of your affirmation and thinking. The affirmation, "I am whole, perfect, strong, powerful, loving, harmonious and happy", will bring about harmonious conditions.

The reason for this is because the affirmation is in strict accordance with the Truth, and when truth appears every form of error or discord must necessarily disappear. You have found that the "I" is spiritual, it must necessarily then always be no less than perfect, the affirmation. "I am whole, perfect, strong, powerful, loving, harmonious and happy" is therefore an exact scientific statement. Whatever you desire for yourself, affirm it for others, and it will help you both. We reap what we sow. If we send out thoughts of love and health, they return to us like bread cast upon the waters...

10. Abundance is a natural law of the Universe. The evidence of this law is conclusive; we see it on every hand. Everywhere Nature is lavish, wasteful, and extravagant.

The man who understands that there is no effect without an adequate cause thinks impersonally. He gets down to bedrock facts regardless of consequences.

Thought is the connecting link between the Infinite and the finite, between the Universal and the individual. Constructive thought must necessarily be creative, but creative thought must be harmonious, and this eliminates all destructive or competitive thought.

Exercise: Select a blank space on the wall, or any other convenient spot, from where you usually sit, mentally draw a black horizontal line about six inches long, try to see the line as plainly as though it were painted on the wall; now mentally draw two vertical lines connecting with this horizontal line at either end; now draw another horizontal line connecting with the two vertical lines; now you have a square. Try to see the square perfectly; when you can do so draw a circle within the square; now place a point in the center of the circle; now draw the point toward you about 10 inches; now you have a cone on a square base; you will remember that your work was all in black; change it to white, to red, to yellow.

Many fail because, they do not understand the law; there is no link to universal mind; they have not formed the connection. The remedy is a conscious recognition of the law of attraction with the intention of bringing the best into existence for a definite purpose. If done rightly, thought will correlate with its object (what you want) and bring it into manifestation, because thought is a product of the spiritual man, and spirit is the creative Principle of the Universe.

11. While every effect is the result of a cause, the effect in turn becomes a cause, which creates other effects, which in turn create still other causes; so that when you put the law of attraction into operation you must remember that you are starting a train of causation for good or otherwise which may have endless possibilities. We are first to believe that our desire has already been fulfilled, its accomplishment will then follow. This is a concise direction for making use of the creative power of thought by impressing on the Universal subjective mind, the particular thing which we desire as an already existing fact.

This conception is also elaborated upon by Swedenborg in his doctrine of correspondences; and a still greater teacher has said, "What things soever ye desire, when ye pray, believe that ye receive them, and ye shall have them." (Mark 11:24) The difference of the tenses in this passage is remarkable. "Faith is the substance of things hoped for, the evidence of things unseen." The Law of Attraction is the Law by which Faith is brought into manifestation. This law has eliminated the elements of uncertainty and caprice from men's lives and substituted law, reason, and certitude.

Exercise: Concentrate on the quotation from Ancient Scripture, "Whatsoever things ye desire, when ye pray, believe that ye receive them and ye shall have them"; notice that there is no limitation, "Whatsoever things" is very definite and implies that the only limitation which is placed upon us in our ability to think, to be equal to the occasion, to rise to the emergency, to remember that Faith is not a shadow, but a substance, "the substance of things hoped for, the evidence of things not seen."

12. "You must first have the knowledge of your power; second, the courage to dare; third, the faith to do." It is the combination of Thought and Love which forms the irresistible force, called the law of attraction. All natural laws are irresistible, the law of Gravitation, or Electricity, or any other law operates with mathematical exactitude.

The intention governs the attention. Things are created in the mental or spiritual world before they appear in the outward act or event by the simple process of governing our thought forces today, we help create the events which will come into our lives in the future, perhaps even tomorrow.

Exercise: Get into the same relaxed state in the same position as you were previously; let go, both mentally and physically; always do this; never try to do any mental work under pressure; see that there are no tense muscles or nerves, that you are entirely comfortable. Now realize your unity with omnipotence; get into touch with this power, come into a deep and vital understanding, appreciation, and realization of the fact that your ability to think is your ability to act upon the Universal Mind, and bring it into manifestation, realize that it will meet any and every requirement; that you have exactly the same potential ability which any individual ever did have or ever will have, because each is but an expression or manifestation of the One, all are parts of the whole, there is no difference in kind or quality, the only difference being one of degree.

13. Part Thirteen which follows tells why the dreams of the dreamer come true. It explains the law of causation by which dreamers, inventors, authors, financiers, bring about the realization of their desires. It explains the law by which the thing pictured upon our mind eventually becomes our own. Every individual who ever advanced a new idea, whether a Columbus, a Darwin, a Galileo, a Fulton or an Emerson, was subjected to ridicule or persecution; so that this objection should receive no serious consideration; but, on the contrary, we should carefully consider every fact which is brought to our attention; by doing this we will more readily ascertain the law upon which it is based.

In creating a Mental Image or an Ideal, we are projecting a thought into the Universal Substance (The Whole) from which all things are created. This means that recognition of Universal Substance brings about realization and a connection. When this tremendous fact begins to permeate your consciousness, when you really come into a realization of the fact that you (not your body, but the Ego), the "I," the spirit which thinks is an integral part of the great whole, that it is the same in substance, in quality, in kind, that the Creator could create nothing different from Himself, you will also be able to say, "The Father and I are one" and you will come into an understanding of the beauty, the grandeur, & the transcendental opportunities which have been placed at your disposal.

Exercise: Make use of the principle, recognize the fact that you are a part of the whole, and that a part must be the same in kind and quality as the whole; the only difference there can possibly by, is in degree. If connected and in tune, then your thoughts are mind are in fact heard and received by Creation.

14. Thought is a spiritual activity and is therefore endowed with creative power. This does not mean that some thought is creative, but that all thought is creative. Mankind is part of all there is. Our mind is connected to our body and to Spirit. Each cell is born, reproduces itself, dies and is absorbed. The maintenance of health and life itself depends upon the constant regeneration of these cells. This change or growth of thought or enhancement of your mental attitude will not only bring you the material things which are necessary for your highest and best welfare, but will bring health and harmonious conditions generally. Imagine over time that your body, organs, and cells being are being regenerated to perfection and the old cells being cast away. In the same way, your power to attract the best from the world may operate if you are harmonious in mind, constructive in word and deed, and into action.

Exercise: Concentrate on Harmony, and when I say concentrate, I mean all that the word implies; concentrate so deeply, so earnestly, that you will be conscious of nothing but harmony. Remember, we learn by doing. Reading these lessons will get you nowhere. It is in the practical application that the value consists AND Slow down your pace for one month. Wake up earlier, do things efficiently without haste, allow others to pass you by in person or in your car. Be courteous with a smile. Each day, praise or complement somebody. This will change your world view within a month.

15. Difficulties and obstacles, indicate that we are either refusing to let go of what we no longer need, or refusing to accept what we require. A scientific example is of a tiny parasite that adapts and grows wings rather than dying. In this way, people always have the inclination to adapt, improve and innovate. The question is when and how? Unfortunately, many times we are taught the same harmful lesson over and over until we are forced to take risk and truly change. To truly change, we must alter mind and spirit with our thoughts. In order to possess vitality, thought must be impregnated with love. Love is a product of the emotions. Therefore, thought and constructive emotion such as: Love, Gratitude,

Faith and even Hope will most certainly stimulate the forces of the universe to assist you in your journey. This leads to the inevitable conclusion that if we wish to express abundance in our lives, we can afford to think abundance only, and as words are only thoughts taking form, we must be especially careful to use nothing but constructive and harmonious language, which when finally crystallized into objective forms, will prove to our advantage. This wonderful power of clothing thoughts in the form of words is what differentiates man from the rest of the animal kingdom. Words are thoughts and are therefore an invisible and invincible power which will finally objectify themselves in the form they are given. Overall, we may use constructive thinking and speech to master our destiny. To overcome error thoughts, we may use a conscious realization of the fact that Truth invariably destroys error. We do not have to laboriously shovel the darkness out; all that is necessary is to turn on the light. The same principle applies to every form of negative thought.

Exercise: Concentrate on Insight; take your accustomed relaxed position and focus the thought on the fact that to have knowledge of the creative power of thought does not mean to possess the art of thinking. Let the thought dwell on the fact that knowledge does not apply itself. Our actions are not governed by knowledge, but by custom, precedent and habit. i.e. (Mental and Physical). That the only way we can get ourselves to apply knowledge is by a determined conscious effort in doing something effectively with focus. Call to mind the fact that knowledge unused passes from the mind, that the value of the information is in the application of the principle; continue this line of thought until you gain sufficient insight to formulate a definite program for applying this principle to your own particular problem.

16. Wealth should then never be desired as an end, but simply as a means of accomplishing an end. Success is contingent upon a higher goal ideal than the mere accumulation of riches, and he who aspires to such success must formulate an ideal for which he is willing to strive. Therefore, the essence of what we will do with wealth must be codified into a purpose of mind and desire. One early 20th century author stated that he posed this question to a multi-millionaire with a railroad empire.... "Did you actually vision to yourself the whole thing? I mean, did you, or could you, really close your eyes and see the tracks? And the trains running? And hear

the whistles blowing? Did you go as far as that?" "Yes." "How clearly?" "Very clearly."

Visualization must, of course, be directed by the will; we are to visualize exactly what we want; we must be careful not to let the imagination run riot. Thought is the plastic material with which we build images of our growing conception of life. Use determines its existence. We can form our own mental images, through our own interior processes of thought regardless of the thoughts of others, regardless of exterior conditions, regardless of environment of every kind, and it is by the exercise of this power that we can control our own destiny, body, mind and soul. The result will depend upon the mental images from which it emanates; this will depend upon the depth of the impression, the predominance of the idea, the clarity of the vision, the boldness of the image.

Exercise: Try to bring yourself to a realization of the important fact that harmony and happiness are states of consciousness and do not depend upon the possession of things. A billionaire can be paralyzed by fear of losing it all. A pauper can have the strength and courage of a Navy Seal. Things are effects and come as a consequence of correct mental states. So that if we desire material possession of any kind our chief concern should be to acquire the mental attitude which will bring about the result desired. This mental attitude is brought about by a realization of our spiritual nature and our unity with the Universal Mind which is the substance of all things. This realization will bring about everything which is necessary for our complete enjoyment. This is scientific or correct thinking. When we succeed in bringing about this mental attitude it is comparatively easy to realize our desire as an already accomplished fact; when we can do this we shall have found the "Truth" which makes us "free" from every lack or limitation of any kind.

"Scientific thinking is a recognition of the creative nature of spiritual energy and our ability to control it."

17. We are accustomed to look upon the Universe with a lens of five senses, and from these experiences our anthropomorphic conceptions originate, but true conceptions are only secured by spiritual insight. This insight requires a quickening of the vibrations of the Mind, and is only secured when the mind is continuously concentrated in a given direction.

The subconscious mind may be aroused and brought into action in any direction and made to serve us for any purpose, by concentration. All mental discovery and attainment are the result of desire plus concentration; desire is the strongest mode of action; the more persistent the desire, the more authoritative the revelation. Desire added to concentration will wrench any secret from nature.

Vibration is the action of thought; it is vibration which reaches out and attracts the material necessary to construct and build. There is nothing mysterious concerning the power of thought; concentration simply implies that consciousness can be focalized to the point where it becomes identified with the object of its attention. Always concentrate on the ideal as an already existing fact; this is the life principle which goes forth and sets in motion those causes which guide, direct and bring about the necessary relation, which eventually manifest in form.

Exercise: Concentrate as nearly as possible in accordance with the method outlined in this lesson; let there be no conscious effort or activity associated with your purpose. Relax completely, avoid any thought of anxiety as to results. Remember that power comes through repose. Let the thought dwell upon your objective and ideal pictures, until you ARE completely identified with it, until you are conscious of nothing else.
Lesson: If you wish to eliminate fear, concentrate on courage, if you wish to eliminate lack, concentrate on abundance, and if you wish to eliminate disease, concentrate on health.

"Intuition usually comes in the Silence; great minds seek solitude frequently." Dr. C. Haanel

18. Thought is the invisible link by which the individual comes into communication with the Universal, the finite with the Infinite, the seen with the Unseen. Thought is the magic by which the human is transformed into a being who thinks and knows and feels and acts. Growth is conditioned on reciprocal action, and we find that on the mental plane like attracts like, that mental vibrations respond only to the extent of their vibratory harmony. It is clear, therefore, that thoughts of abundance and health will respond only to similar thoughts. The connecting link between the individual and the Universal is Thought, and Love and Inner Harmony (a

powerful emotion and feeling) is what fuels thought into manifestation or cooperation from the universe.

Exercise: Concentrate upon your power to create; seek insight, perception; try to find a logical basis for the faith which is in you. Let the thought dwell on the fact that the physical man lives and moves and has his being in the sustainer of all organic life air, that he must breathe to live. Then let the thought rest on the fact that the spiritual man also lives and moves and has his being in a similar but subtler energy upon which he must depend for life, and that as in the physical world, no life assumes form until after a seed (design) is sown, and no higher fruit than that of the parent stock can be produced; so in the spiritual world no effect can be produced until the seed is sown and the fruit will depend upon the nature of the seed, so that the results which you secure depend upon your perception of law in the mighty domain of causation, the highest evolution of human consciousness.

19. In the Moral World we find the same law; we speak of good and evil, but Good is a reality, something tangible, while Evil is found to be simply a negative condition, the absence of Good. We know that the ability of the individual to think in constructive ways is his ability to act upon the Universal Mind and convert it into dynamic mind, or mind in motion. We have then come to know that Mind is the only principle which is operative in the physical, mental, moral and spiritual world.

Exercise: Concentrate, and when I use the word concentrate, I mean all that the word implies; become so absorbed in the object of your thought that you are conscious of nothing else, and do this a few minutes every day. You take the necessary time to eat in order that the body may be nourished, why not take the time to assimilate your mental food? Let the thought rest on the fact that appearances are deceptive. The earth is not flat, neither is it stationary; the sky is not a dome, the sun does not move, the stars are not small specks of light, and matter which was once supposed to be fixed has been found to be in a state of perpetual flux. Try to realize that the day is fast approaching -- its dawn is now at hand -- when modes of thought and action must be adjusted to rapidly increasing knowledge of the operation of eternal principles.

20. God is Spirit. Spirit is the Creative Principle of the Universe. Man is made in the image and likeness of God. Man is therefore a spiritual being. The only activity which spirit possesses is the power to think. Thinking is therefore a creative process. All form is therefore the result of the thinking process. When you begin to perceive that the essence of the Universal is within yourself -- is you -- you begin to do things; you begin to feel your power; it is the fuel which fires the imagination; which lights the torch of inspiration; which gives vitality to thought; which enables you to connect with all the invisible forces of the Universe. It is this power which will enable you to plan fearlessly, to execute masterfully. This "breath of life" is a superconscious reality.

It is the essence of the "I am." It is pure "Being" or Universal Substance, and our conscious unity with it enables us to localize it, and thus exercise the powers of this creative energy. Thought which is in harmony with the Universal Mind will result in corresponding conditions. Thought which is destructive or discordant will produce corresponding results. You may use thought constructively or destructively, but the immutable law will not allow you to plant a thought of one kind and reap the fruit of another.

You may have all the wealth in the world, but unless you recognize it and make use of it, it will have no value; so with your spiritual wealth: unless you recognize it and use it, it will have no value.

Lesson: Inspiration is from within. The Silence is necessary, the senses must be stilled, the muscles relaxed, repose cultivated. When you have thus come into possession of a sense of poise and power you will be ready to receive the information or inspiration or wisdom which may be necessary for the development of your purpose.

Exercise: Go into the Silence and concentrate on the fact that "In him we live and move and have our being" is literally and scientifically exact! That you ARE because He IS, that if He is Omnipresent He must be in you. That if He is all in all you must be in Him! That He is Spirit and you are made in "His image and likeness" and that the only difference between His spirit and your spirit is one of degree, that a part must be the same in kind and quality as the whole. When you can realize this clearly you will have found the secret of the creative power of thought, you will have found the origin of both good and evil, you will have found the secret of the wonderful power of concentration, you will have found the key to the solution of every problem whether physical, financial, or environmental.

21. "A Master-Mind thinks big thoughts. The creative energies of mind find no more difficulty in handling large situations, than small ones." Everything which we hold in our consciousness for any length of time becomes impressed upon our subconscious and so becomes a pattern which the creative energy will wave into our life and environment. This is the secret of the wonderful power of prayer The real secret of power is consciousness of power. The Universal Mind is unconditional; therefore, the more conscious we become of our unity with this mind, the less conscious we shall become of conditions and limitations, and as we become emancipated or freed from conditions we come into a realization of the unconditional. We have become free! Thus, prayer, meditation, and focused thought can be extremely effective in reaching your heights.

It is no easy matter to change the mental attitude, but by persistent effort it may be accomplished. The mental attitude is patterned after the mental pictures which have been photographed on the brain. If you do not like the pictures, destroy the negatives and create new pictures; this is the art of visualization. The Divine Mind makes no exceptions to favor any individual; but when the individual understands and realizes his Unity with the Universal principle he will appear to be favored because he will have found the source of all health, all wealth, and all power.

Exercise: Concentrate on the Truth. Try to realize that the Truth shall make you free, that is, nothing can permanently stand in the way of your perfect success when you learn to apply the scientifically correct thought methods and principles. Realize that you are externalizing in your environment your inherent soul potencies. Realize that the Silence offers an ever-available and almost unlimited opportunity for awakening the highest conception of Truth. Try to comprehend that Omnipotence itself is absolute silence, all else is change, activity, limitation. Silent thought concentration is therefore the true method of reaching, awakening, and then expressing the wonderful potential power of the world within.

22. Thoughts are spiritual seeds, which, when planted in the subconscious mind, have a tendency to sprout and grow, but unfortunately the fruit is frequently not to our liking. To remain healthy and regain health, we must increase the inflow and distribution of vital energy throughout the system, and this can only be done by eliminating thoughts of fear, worry, care, anxiety, jealousy, hatred, and every other destructive thought, which tend to tear down and destroy optimal health. It is through the law of vibration that the mind exercises this control over the body. We know that every mental action is a vibration, and we know that all form is simply a mode of motion, a rate of vibration. Therefore, any given vibration immediately modifies every atom in the body, every life cell is affected and an entire chemical change is made in every group of life cells. Through cooperation with our body, cell life and regeneration can be maintained at its highest levels.

Exercise: Concentrate on Tennyson's beautiful lines "Speak to Him, thou, for He hears, and spirit with spirit can meet, Closer is He than breathing, and nearer than hands and feet." Then try to realize that when you do "Speak to Him" you are in touch with Omnipotence. This realization and recognition of this Omnipresent power will quickly destroy any and every form of sickness or suffering and substitute harmony and perfection. Of course we should see a doctor if they can remove an infection and fix a problem. Thus, we should cooperate with all those available who should help us in a truthful manner while also cooperating with our bodies and spirit to heal, regenerate, and reach abundance. You will then more readily appreciate the ideal man, the man made in the image and likeness of God, and you will more readily appreciate the all originating Mind that forms, upholds, sustains, originates, and creates all there is.

23. One of the highest laws of success is service. Service to yourself and to humanity. It is inevitable that the entertainment of positive, constructive and unselfish thoughts should have a far-reaching effect for good. Compensation is the keynote of the universe. Nature is constantly seeking to strike an equilibrium. Where something is sent out something must be received; else there should be a vacuum formed.

You can make a money magnet of yourself, but to do so you must first consider how you can make money for other people. We make money by making friends, and we enlarge our circle of friends by making money for them, by helping them, by being of service to them. The first law of success then is service, and this in turn is built on integrity and justice. Keep in mind, generous thoughts filled with strength and vitality. Giving without expectation will form a vacuum which must be filled. Therefore, the laws of cause and effect will favor you with your sincere assistance and service to others.

Helping Others Mentally: If you desire to help someone, to destroy some form of lack, limitation or error, the correct method is not to think of the person whom you wish to help; the intention to help them is entirely sufficient, as this puts you in mental touch with the person. Then drive out of your own mind any belief of lack, limitation, disease, danger, difficulty or whatever the trouble might be. As soon as you have succeeded is doing this the result will have been accomplished, and the person will be free.

Attention develops concentration, and concentration develops Spiritual Power, and Spiritual Power is the mightiest force in existence. The power of attention is called concentration; this power is directed by the will; for this reason we must refuse to concentrate or think of anything except the things we desire. "Spirituality" is quite "practical," very "practical," intensely "practical." It teaches that Spirit is the Real Thing, the Whole Thing, and that Matter is but plastic stuff, which Spirit is able to create, mould, manipulate, and fashion to its will. Spirituality is the most "practical" thing in the world -- the only really and absolutely "practical" thing that there is!

Exercise: Concentrate on the fact that man is not a body with a spirit, but a spirit with a body, and that it is for this reason that his desires are incapable of any permanent satisfaction in anything not spiritual. Money is therefore of no value except to bring about the conditions which we desire, and these conditions are necessarily harmonious. Harmonious conditions necessitate sufficient supply, so that if there appears to be any lack, we should realize that the idea or soul of money is service, and as this thought takes form, channels of supply will be opened, and you will have the satisfaction of knowing that spiritual methods are entirely practical.

24. If you have practiced each of the exercises a few minutes every day, as suggested, you will have found that you can get out of life exactly what you wish by first putting into life that which you wish. Every form of concentration, forming Mental Images, Constructive Argument, and Autosuggestion are all simply methods by which you are enabled to realize the Truth.

When you master these steps, you will have mastered TRUTH. The method for removing this error is to go into the Silence and know the Truth; as all mind is one mind, you can do this for yourself or anyone else. If you have learned to form mental images of the conditions desired, this will be the easiest and quickest way to secure results; if not, results can be accomplished by argument, by the process of convincing yourself absolutely of the truth of your statement.

The absolute truth is that the "I" is perfect and complete; the real "I" is spiritual and can therefore never be less than perfect; it can never have any lack, limitation, or disease. The flash of genius does not have origin in the molecular motion of the brain; it is inspired by the ego, the spiritual "I" which is one with the Universal Mind, and it is our ability to recognize this Unity which is the cause of all inspiration, all genius.

Most people understand this word "GOD" to mean something outside of themselves; while exactly the contrary is the fact. It is our very life. Without it we would be dead. We would cease to exist. The minute the spirit leaves the body, our bodies are as nothing. Therefore, spirit is really, all there is of us. When the truth of this statement is realized, understood, and appreciated, you will have come into mystical possession of the Master's Secret.

Now, the only activity which the spirit possesses is the power to think. Therefore, thought must be creative, because spirit is creative. This creative power is impersonal and your ability to think is your ability to control it and make use of it for the benefit of yourself and others. The conditions with which you meet in the world without are invariably the result of the conditions obtaining in the world within, therefore it follows with scientific accuracy that by holding the perfect ideal in mind you can bring about ideal conditions in your environment. What is meant by thinking? Clear, decisive, calm, deliberate, sustained thought with a definite end in view. What will be the result? You will also be able to say, "It is not I that doeth the works, but the 'Father' that dwelleth within me, He doeth the works." You will come to know that the "Father" is the Universal Mind and that the Essence of the Supreme really and truly does dwell within you, in other words, you will come to know that the wonderful promises made in Scripture are fact, not fiction, and can be demonstrated by anyone having sufficient understanding.

Each student should focus on these steps:

1. What are your desires? Define them.
2. Are you willing to write out what you "want to be" and what you want for yourself. Can you be specific? Can you ask for more that you ever believed you could achieve?
3. Can you envision your ideal circumstances? Try and see them vividly.
4. Do you have the ability to select a definite ideal, goal and purpose to materialize? Can you specify what you desire in concrete forms written on paper and in the spoken word?
5. Are you willing to engage a harmonious relationship with the world and universe? Can you cultivate a thankful heart and practice/express gratitude on a daily basis?
6. Are you willing to take action? Can you bolding begin your dream? Are you willing to ask others for insight, cooperation and help?
7. Are you willing to focus and concentrate on constructive ideals and goals? Can you give your attention to one primary aim "all day every day"? Can you give your all – day in and day out to your ideal or goal?
8. Can you affirm to yourself verbally and with mental images the successful completion of your desires?
9. Are you willing to consider yourself worthy of having a fuller and richer life. Can you arrange your affairs so that you can receive what you earn or take delivery of gifts of grace and prosperity.
10. Is it possible for you to believe that you have possession of your desires NOW and IN THIS MOMENT as if you actually HAVE them in MIND.... Can you imagine yourself owning, being, or having what you really want. Why not?

11. Can you live, speak and act in a proactive way in which your words, thoughts and actions are in concordance with prosperity, abundance, and peace.
12. Are you willing to be grateful for the things you have and the things you do not have yet?
13. Are you willing to engage your desires and passions with emotions of love and gratitude.
14. Can you practice seeing what you want in your minds eye on a regular basis.

24-28 - Module Twendy-Five Through Twenty Eight – Observations

The wisdom in the first 24 MODULES must be analyzed in the totality of life's circumstances. Each person is unique with varying talents and abilities, and ALL people have talent and abilities to be cultivated and honed on the mental, spiritual, and physical planes. All persons have a divine right to live, prosper and love in an abundant and creative environment. All things are possible with desire, faith, love, harmonious action and constructive thinking. It should be remembered that these steps below are important in our quest for excellence and peace. Take the best ideas from the list below and use them to improve your life: [xl]

1. The use of concentration and focus in your endeavors is vital. "Right Now" is the only moment in time that you HAVE to LIVE and to be of service. Not yesterday and not tomorrow.
2. Waste must be eliminated or transformed. Non-useful mental energies, thoughts and actions should be processed, avoided, or eliminated. Further, the body is Your temple; thus, you should consider the most constructive engagement of activities to revitalize and improve your body, mind and soul.

3. Cycles of growth and life occur. You may go through phases of struggle, challenge, strengthening, and transcendence. Analyze the cycles of your life. Your growth leads to greater abilities, lessons learned, & knowledge.
4. Your body desires "life force". One of the ways to achieve greater life force is through breathing, meditation, and exercise. There are multitudes of activities and exercise that induce breathing, rejuvenation and the building of mental, spiritual, and physical fitness. It is your job to contemplate how to best accomplish this.
5. Staying connected with the source and forces of the Universe requires willingness. This connection also affords you stronger abilities to propel mind thought into the universe through prayer, contemplation, meditation or concentration.
6. The character of your thought is YOU. What you think is your reality. Your perception and peace of mind is governed by the quality and harmonious nature of your thought.
7. Love and spiritual harmony is the missing ingredient to success. Your thoughts attract like thoughts. Your thoughts and desires mixed with feeling-emotion and blended with love will manifest opportunities and blessings. You will serve humanity and achieve your highest good with the use of Love Energy and Love Thought. Sometimes love energy can be equated with your sexual magnetism also. The good news is that sexual magnetism and love energy can be harnessed and directed into your relationships, success, growth and other areas in a constructive way.
8. You determine your conscious relation to "ALL that IS" including people, places, things & the universal spirit. Your conscious thoughts are vibrations that surround you and vibrations sent out into the world. Harmonious thoughts will attract people toward you.
9. Blessings, focus, praise and gratitude directed toward anything or anyone will tend to bring that person or thing into your life. Thus, what you focus on expands. What is not important to you will tend to leave you, and this includes people, things, spirit force, or different types of thinking.
10. Surround yourself with experts and those who understand your desires. Form win-win relationships. As you give, you will receive in return.
11. Be aware of opportunities. People will offer proposals and ideas. You must be ready and willing to receive or use them.

12. Communication is key. Learn to speak, write, and communicate with others about your goals. Learn to ask for help, follow through, and give and receive to facilitate a more abundant life.
13. Learn to love yourself as worthy of all the good that the universe has to offer. Speak, act and do "AS IF" you are worthy. Do NOT discuss your past difficulties, faults or other negative circumstances. If you must, do it with a spiritual advisor or analyst.
14. For specific goals and desires, try to relax and imagine the specific desire as you want it, as if you have it, detailing the picture on your mental screen, capturing the emotion, and harvesting the essence of the desire. Feel the joy of fulfilling the desire and love the thought of it unfolding. Hold the thought images clearly and often to further develop your thoughts.
15. Remember that truth can be more than meets the eye. Try and see beyond what is apparent. Sometimes the eventual outcomes of your plans are better that you could have imagined.
16. Action is the catalyst to propel your mental and spiritual advances. As you enhance and advance at all spiritual levels, your intuition and mind thoughts will guide you to do more and more toward the fulfillment of your desires. You will achieve things one by one effectively which leads you to your highest good.
17. Waking up from the 3rd dimensional dream-state world and recognizing you are finally in the 4th dimension of co-creation with the universe is the fruit of our research, reading, and exercise of these principles. You are now master of your destiny in harmony and cooperation with the source of ALL and the universe.
18. Flowing from all of these steps and suggestions, these blessings will allow you to guide and help others. You give of yourself & teach others so that you can keep your flow with the universe and fullness of life.

The Elemental Mind and Body

It is somewhat essential to know that we are not merely this visible body, but have a vital body to charge it with energy, a desire body to spend this force, a mind to guide our exertions in channels of reason, and that we are virgin spirits enmeshed in a threefold veil as egos.

It is also interesting to contemplate that the physical body is the material counterpart of the Divine Spirit, that the vital body is a replica of the Life Spirit, and that the desire body is the shadow of the Human Spirit, the mind forming the link between the threefold spirit and the threefold body.

Even when a seeker analyzes the various cultures around the world, you may find that the soul, mind, self, and spirit may be made up of various parts.

"I AM NOT MY EGO" is a saying that most of us would agree with. There is something deeper. Something in the Heart that you might refer to as "ME" or your higher spirit.

As with Ancient Celtic Faiths, the soul or spirit is an inherently complex manifestation. We will not go into depth here, but it is important to consider that the spirit includes: Soul Essence, Animating Breath of Life or Silver Chord, The Body Perception, The Shadow Geist, The Hame Skin, The Fetch Opposite or Feminine, The Mind Emotion, the Memory or Sippe Primal Memories of Ancestry, The Wit 5 Senses of perception, The Will of Boldness and Creation, the Mood of Base Emotions, and the Wode of Higher passions.

In putting this all together, there is the self that wills to survive and attain, the spirit that desires creation and natural expression, and the Mind which assists with memory and function on a conscious and subconscious level.

Many writers have implied that we must maintain balance with the various parts of our soul, self, and mind much like we maintain balance with Body, Mind and Spirit. Some writers refer to the Vital or Elemental body as the part of you that serves you in many ways with confidence, creation, support and energy. Much like an imaginary childhood friend, this vital or elemental body is always there to help you, meet with you, talk with you, and assist you. It is your job to nurture it and keep it healthy. [xli]

Some Observations

It seems that the whole dynamic message contained in prosperity teachings hinges on the concept of ideas, mind and mind stuff that can propel energy or communication. However, to work with the forms of mind stuff, the individual consciousness must have a stream of something called thought. Random thought can be a waste of energy and time for all involved. However, thought that is inspired by ideas has great power.

Thought with purpose, feeling, and concentration is even more energized.

As we must remember, when we connect to and activate the supernatural MIND within, we are inspired with the divine ideas of: innovation, change, growth, and creation. Acting and seizing upon this new 6th sense that is tied to your natural expressive self is the KEY to right livelihood, effort, and action. Stop fighting and resisting growth and your potential. You and Your constructive dreams and ideas are your purpose and wealth. It is an unlimited supply of being and creative substance.

When a person stops struggling and quits the debating society, SOMETHING HAPPENS. An openness and willingness appears. It is an energy of great force. Hope is good because it signifies an openness to surrender to something greater which many persons refer to the supernatural energy of faith power. To transcend struggle and hope is to begin singing the praises of creation. Discouragement, frustration, blame and justified anger drain great amounts of spiritual energy from anyone. To choose a new world view takes great effort but this choice soon becomes a skill of discernment. To develop this skill, we must overcome laziness and self-anointed victimhood as soon as possible. However, much like a mental gymnasium, any man or woman can begin a shift of consciousness with practice and open-mindedness. A consciousness with a bedrock foundation of gratitude, acceptance, peace , willingness, and desire can lead to a real shift toward tangible belief and conviction.

It is not the quantity of spirituality; it is the quality of Faith and Knowingness. Even if part of your conscious has doubt of fear, the small and unshakable foundation of faith will immunize your SELF from false appearances. As we all know, a tiny amount of light prevents darkness from existing and your inner light will invariably grow if you allow it and are willing to receive it. Meet the universe half-way with good cheer and a world view backed by love, thanks and praise, and the heavens will continue to shower you with abundance and opportunity to serve humanity.

The reason for studying these concepts is this. You can render no greater service to humanity than to make the most of yourself. Without a proper view of yourself and the world of opportunity in life, you may never begin to engage life and living in a way to maximize the fullness of your existence. Because poverty and ignorance generally interfere with freedom and love, we begin to ask all who read these teachings if you are ready to recreate your world and reinvent your soul essence.

On this physical plane, we see that like causes do IN FACT cause like effects. Thus, if we desire a certain result, we use the method or formula that proves most effective. So, most people recognize that a recipe has certain ingredients, but most in this world do not comprehend that CREATION and TRUE Success has certain mental and spiritual ingredients also.

Nature itself is responsive to your mind. It is an undeniable fact. The original or primordial substance can be molded by spiritual mind. Because we have not achieved the advanced stages of our spiritual evolution, we are working now in the beginning phases of cognitive transcendence and mastery, but even at this stage, an average person can become endowed with more power that then had ever hoped and wished for.

Without perfect manifestation, we are using the strategies that allow advance creation. These tactics are spiritual in nature, but dramatically speed up progress on both the physical and spiritual plane for anyone who is willing to use them.

- Begin NOW to cultivate your burning desires and life's purpose. (Things that you truly want to do and are willing to commit wholeheartedly to). You can also refer to this as your intentions and goals. Make a list of things you want to achieve and begin honing you plans and objectives. Make a list of things about yourself that you want to improve, and begin to think about these also.
- Simply allow yourself believe in one Intelligent Substance where you express thankful acknowledgement. The universe wants to help you, it has unlimited supply, and only desires your cooperation by meeting it ½ way.
- Realize that what you desire is available to be yours with Grateful Heartfelt Emotion and Faith and you only need to say the word to have it begin to become manifest.

- Form a blueprint of what you desire in your mind and on your mental picture screen. See it each and every day and allow it to be cultivated and specific in nature.
- Give you attention wholly to prosperity and thoughts of creation.
- Since Belief is All Important, it best serves you to stay away from people, places and entertainment that you know will interfere with your Constructive Path and Affirmative Consciousness. Quit struggling and start: Doing and Being.
- Do all you can each day without haste or hurry that leads to the completion of your goals or desires. Do things one at a time as best you can.
- Do not focus on the poverty and ills of the world. Take action to protect and improve yourself. You will then be able to help others all you want after you have become truly prosperous on the inside and out.

Taoism

The Classic Text of the ***Dao De Jing by* Lao Tzu** - Taoism**, Tao or DAO** – The Loge respects the teachings that were brought to the West by Alexander the Great after the exposure to the oriental wisdom of India.

Taoism could be the most ancient of the Chinese Religious Philosophies possibly dating farther back than 3000 BC. The philosophy has quite amazing undertones of tuning in with nature both externally and internally. Because Tao is considered the underlying force or spirit of everything, the use of or invoking of the word Tao has a very spiritual essence. Many writers refer to Tao much like Westerners would refer to the "power of the universe" or "the forces of nature". It can also be said that a Taoist is a Spiritual Alchemist who believes that the physical and spiritual body is at one with ALL as the internal mind is corresponding to the external all.

Taoists accept that the Tao is all permeating, a great oneness from which all things emanate. Moreover, a Taoist generally believes in the Eastern Philosophy that each of us is a microcosm of the great ALL where the power of Yin and Yang are involved. Ying and Yang may be discusses as differences in thought such as reality and illusion or logic versus emotion. Hermetic thought may more distinguish Yin and Yang by discussing the gender related aspects of Yin and Yang such as: the feminine Yin power of creativity.

With the All Permeating Force and Energy, Taoists believe that we are in an unformed and natural state. Thus, our cooperation with the Tao allows co-creation of our lives. As such, our thinking and "way of life" actually creates our world. Also, Taoists are adherents to variations of breathing exercises which involves bringing in life energy. This is also a pathway to become more at-one with the ALL in breath , life, silence or thinking. Naturally, Taoists enjoy breathing exercises where the vitality of life is inhaled while exhaling the impurities of the body and mind.

Taoists lean toward natural expression. This belief coincides with flowing with life instead of fighting against it. Many say that the Taoist life involves more spontaneous and free conduct. Moreover, Neo-Taoists seem to have a great focus on a stricter Authenticity in living and being true to your nature.

Additionally, emptiness in Taoism is something that brings us closer to Tao. For example: moving aside the racing thoughts of our daily life, becoming still & relaxed, and listening to our heart or spirit.

Because Taoism is always open to change, it is considered an optimistic philosophy. Personal change can also be facilitated by putting yourself into another's position mentally and emotionally to see their perspective. Further, it may be healthy to analyze our perception of others to evaluate our thinking.

Overall, expressing your true nature and talents allows the practitioner to be in tune with the TAO. Using opposing forces to your advantage is one of the key elements to the Mental and Physical TAO Philosophy. This is quite similar to the Egyptian and Greek points of the Kyballion Hermetic System. As such, Taoism is a preemptive philosophy that aspires to mitigate problems or optimize success by taking action sooner rather than later.

Like the Myth of the Yellow Emperor who backed off from micromanaging his people, Taoist beliefs suggest that non-interference with people can actually allow them to flower and unfold better than our expectations toward their true place or "right livelihood".   This philosophical aspect of Taoism emphasizes various themes found in the *Tao Te Ching* (道德經) such as: naturalness, vitality, peace, "non-action" (*wu wei*), purity/emptiness (refinement), harmony, the strength of softness (or flexibility), and in the *Zhuangzi* 《庄子》 such as receptiveness, spontaneity, the relativism of human ways of life, ways of speaking and guiding behavior.

Taoist Core Concepts and Beliefs

1. Tao is the primal-cause of the universe. It is a force that permeates through all life.
2. The Tao surrounds everyone and therefore all people must be aware to find enlightenment.
3. Each practitioner's goal is to harmonize themselves with the Tao.
4. The Taoist scholars view the many gods as manifestations of the one Dao, "*which could not be represented as an image or a particular thing*." Taoists seek solutions to life's challenges through inner meditation and outer observation.
5. Taoists strongly promote vitality through breath exercises. Each person must nurture the *Ch'i* (air, breath) that has been given to them.
6. Development of virtue is one's chief task. The *Three Jewels* of Virtue to be sought out are: compassion, moderation and humility.
7. Taoists follow the art of "*wu wei*," which is to let nature take its course.
8. One should plan in advance and be mindful of consequences
9. A Taoists extends kindness to others, in part because such an action tends to be reciprocated.

10. Taoists believe that "*people are compassionate by nature and inherently good...left to their own devices people will show compassion without expecting a reward.*"
11. The 5 main organs and orifices of the body correspond to the 5 parts of the sky: water, fire, wood, metal and earth.
12. Time is cyclical, not linear as in Western thinking. i.e. cycles of life will occur.

NOTE: TAO is included herein because of the mystic wisdom exchanged in the invasions and battles of Alexander the Great as they entered and left their mark with Greco-Buddhism. With Buddhism beginning in India and Confucian thought flowing through Asia, the Rosicrucian held this wisdom in high esteem. Ancient Taoism and Vedic thought also includes DIESM in the same manner as Hellenistic, Romanic, and Hermetic thought includes the supreme force and energies. Analysis by Magus Incognito and Supreme Magus

Chakras and Eastern Exercises

Chakra is a Sanskrit word that means circle or wheel. For the purposes of this topic, we will focus on the Hindu model As such, other models such as the Chinese, Bon, and Tantric models do exist. In Hinduism, chakras are part of a complex set of ideas related to esoteric anatomy. This particular system may have originated in about the 11th century AD, and rapidly became popular. Chakras are generally explained as energy centers in the spine located at major branchings of the body's nervous system, beginning at the base of the spinal column and moving up to the top of the head, Chakras are considered to be a point or nexus of metaphysical energy of the human body. The primary chakras are commonly described as: [xlii]

- Muladhara (Sanskrit: Mūlādhāra) Lower body - our connection to the earth and the physical plane – Survival and Operation – Color Red
- Swadhisthana (Sanskrit: Svādhisthāna) Reproductive gland region of the body -our creative and procreative urges and drives. – Color Orange

- Manipura (Sanskrit: Manipūra) Stomach/navel - energy center for power and manifestation and desires (location: solar plexus) – Color Yellow
- Anahata (Sanskrit: Anāhata) Heart - energy center for love – Color Green
- Vishuddha (Sanskrit: Viśuddha) Throat - center for expression – Color Blue
- Ajna (Sanskrit: Ājñā) Eyebrow or forehead between brows - our psychic powers – Color Indigo
- Sahasrara (Sanskrit: Sahasrāra) Top of head and crown - connection with the Cosmic or the divine. – Color Violet

If you read the "health exercise" contained in this book, you will see that prayer, breath-work, meditation, visualization, and recognition of health and peace can be taken point-by-point through the body using a quasi-chakra observance system. When doing the Health Exercise in this book, you also imagine a healing light going through each Chakra Region.

Exercise: Sit in a Chair or Lie Down. Close your eyes. Take in air in your nose, hold it for 7 seconds, and let it out of your mouth slowly. Do this at least 3 times to enter a relaxed state. Clench your fists and extend your fingers as far as they will go a few times and put your hands in your lap. Now clear your mind and imagine a peaceful scene such as a mountain meadow with flowers or calm lake. Now, begin with the Top of the head or crown or you can also begin with the Base or Lower body. Go through each of the 7 sections in one direction. The colors are ROY.G.BIV with Red beginning with the Lower Body and the Head/Crown being the Color Violet.

Now, go through all 7 colors "one by one" imaging the color of each chakra and each section of the body. Imaging each color purifying and regenerating the body "one by one". Relax and purify each section of the body "one by one". When you are finished the exercise from Crown to Lower or Lower to Higher, release any impure energy to the universe while taking a few breaths from the nose and blowing out from the mouth. Then, express a mental thanks to the Supreme for the healing energy. Open your eyes.

Native American Spirituality

Because there are and were so many tribes and nations of American Indians in North and Latin America, we are going to use this section to list some contemplative quotes from famous American Indians or their leaders and Chiefs. This section is a necessary observance for the Lodge of Parfaits 1764 in the USA because the Loge de Parfaits was the first Illumined Order with exposure to original American Spirituality.

1) **As John Mohawk most eloquently expressed:** - The natural world is our bible. We don't have chapters and verses; we have trees and fish and animals. The creation is the manifestation of energy through matter. Because the universe is made up of manifestations of energy, the options for that manifestation are infinite. But we have to admit that the way it has manifested itself is organized. In fact, it is the most intricate organization. We can't know how we impact on its law; we can talk only about how its law impacts upon us. We can make no judgment about nature. The Indian sense of natural law is that nature informs us and it is our obligation to read nature as you would a book, to feel nature as you would a poem, to touch nature as you would yourself, to be a part of that and step into its cycles as much as you can.

2) **Big Thunder (Bedagi) Wabanaki Algonquin -** The Great Spirit is in all things, he is in the air we breathe. The Great Spirit is our Father, but the Earth is our Mother. She nourishes us and that which we put into the ground she returns to us....

3) **Black Elk Oglala Sioux Holy Man - 1863-1950 -** You have noticed that everything as Indian does is in a circle, and that is because the Power of the World always works in circles, and everything tries to be round..... The Sky is round, and I have heard that the earth is round like a ball, and so are all the stars. The wind, in its greatest power, whirls. Birds make their nest in circles, for theirs is the same religion as ours.... Even the seasons form a great circle in their changing, and always come back again to where they

were. The life of a man is a circle from childhood to childhood, and so it is in everything where power moves.

4) **Lone Man (Isna-la-wica) Teton Sioux** ... I have seen that in any great undertaking it is not enough for a man to depend simply upon himself.

5) **In his book, *The Earth Shall Weep*, James Wilson expands his thoughts on Native American Creation Myth.:** Yet for all their range and variety, these stories often have a similar feel to them. When you set them alongside the biblical Genesis, the common features suddenly appear in sharp relief; they seem to glow with the newness and immediacy of creation, offering vivid explanations for the behavior of an animal, the shape of a rock or a mountain, which you can still encounter in the here and now. Many tribes and nations call themselves, in their own languages, 'the first people', the 'original people', or the 'real people', and their stories place them firmly in a place of special power and significance...Far from telling them that they are locked out of Eden, the Indians' myths confirm that (unless they have been displaced by European contact and settlement) they still live in the place for which they were made; either the site of their own emergence or creation, or a 'Promised Land' which they have attained through long migration.

6) **Chief Aupumut, Mohican. 1725** - "When it comes time to die, be not like those whose hearts are filled with the fear of death, so when their time comes they weep and pray for a little more time to live their lives over again in a different way. Sing your death song, and die like a hero going home."

7) **Sitting Bull Hunkpapa Sioux** - "I am a red man. If the Great Spirit had desired me to be a white man he would have made me so in the first place. He put in your heart certain wishes and plans, in my heart he put other and different desires. Each man is good in his sight. It is not necessary for Eagles to be Crows. We are poor..but we are free. No white man controls our footsteps. If we must die...we die defending our rights."

Native American Spiritual Exercise:

The Seven Directions of the Medicine Wheel are: North, South, East, West, Above/Heavens, Below/Earth, and within. Various American Tribes have believed that all is interconnected with spirit, nature, mental, and physical. The medicine wheel reminds us to look each day at our sacred balance and to keep inner harmony. Colors were associated with the four nautical directions. This can be done by yourself or in a circle with others. This is typically done outside and in nature. The exercise suggests that we enter the wheel from the East (face the East) which is the direction of renewal and birth. Focus on the East and think of cleansing and oxygenating energy and take a few deep breaths:

1) We ask for the blessings of the direction of the East, the direction of new beginnings, inspiration, and the rising sun.
2) Then to the South, the direction of passion, heat, and enthusiasm
3) Then to West, the place of intuition and inner knowing
4) Then to the North, the place of communication and community
5) Then look below and we send loving energy deep into Mother Earth
6) Then to above and remember that we are connected to all there in the universe and beyond
7) Then within and petition the Great Spirit by asking for THE presence here with us now in this place

Descriptions of the Directions:

North: This is the direction of the Element Earth and the Power of Body. The color is Blue and represents turmoil, challenge, and opportunity. **South**: This is the direction of the Element Fire and the Power of Action. The color is White and it represents Peace and Happiness. **East**: This is the direction of the Element Air and the Power of Mind. The color is RED and the East represents Success and Victory. **West**: This is the direction of the Element Water and the Power of Emotions. The color is Black and represents the death of part of our thinking or exit of the old.
Above/Heavens: This is the direction of Sky and Cosmos. Represents the Zenith. **Below:** This is the direction of Earth, Planet and Sacred Place. Represents Nadir. **Inside/Within:** This is the direction of Spirit Connection. Represents the Soul within.

The 12 Characteristics of Magical and Prosperous People

1. **A purpose driven personality** with a desire to express themselves in the most constructive ways.
2. **A worldview and consciousness of possibility,** prosperity and harmlessness
3. People who are beyond competitive and very creative. Visionaries who strive to see and feel the reality of their dreams.
4. **Gratitude minded** – people with a thankful heart and sincere belief in the goodness of the universe.
5. **Boldness, action oriented**, willing to take calculated risks, and Authentic.
6. **Self Regard** – people who believe that they are worthy of a rich and full life and are willing to work to receive it.
7. **At-Ease – Harmonious mind and thinking**. People willing to cultivate peace of mind and balance in body, mind and spirit.
8. **Love of Fellowship** – willing to help others with time and talent.

9. **Receptivity** - Global & Non-judgmental openness to others' ideas and creativity. Open to inspiration.
10. **A Unique Spirit** – Individualization of soul and spirit. Allowing yourself to become who you are meant to be.
11. **Desire to serve humanity** be being your best. A passion to contribute as an individual to the greater good.
12. **Spiritual Awakenings** - People who have become Spiritually Awake to a higher order of being and work to maintain such a level of thinking, acting and being.

Rosicrucian Exercises with Magical Power

1. Basic Prayers for Memory

The first exercise is basic prayers. An example of a basic prayer might be the Serenity Prayer by Reinhold Niebuhr: "God grant me the serenity to accept the things I cannot change, the courage to change the things I can, and the wisdom to know the difference." Many other prayers are perfectly acceptable for all types of spiritual seekers. Many of us use the Sermon on the Mount, which includes the Lord's Prayer or "Our Father".

2. Fellowship Exercise

The next exercise is seeking wise counsel & fellowship. One of the top types of spiritual practice in the 21st century (also in the 20th century) is seeking out other spiritually minded people who want to grow and heal in a spiritual way. There are two parts to this—you are giving of yourself and you are letting others give to you. For instance, you may be going to a spiritual gathering where you could discuss wisdom literature, the Bible, or some other spiritual literature and sharing your experience about it, sharing your interpretation of it, sharing your strength and hope regarding the discussion or mentoring or counseling or coaching or sponsoring other people. The reward to this is you are giving it away, but you are also teaching it. You are teaching about something even as you are learning about something. Therefore, you are giving it away to keep it. If you give of yourself, invariably, you are receiving the rewards of the universe by trying to help other people who are deeply in need.

3. Active Meditation

The third exercise is Active meditation which involves reading certain meditative literature, absorbing what it means, musing over the literature, thinking about it, and discussing it with other people out loud. Sometimes when you have an active meditation for reading it could be something written like a psalm or a proverb or a Bible passage. You may even have a dictionary available to interpret each word amongst other people, and then you discuss it out loud, but you can read it out loud as well before discussing it. To give you an example, some people may be sitting on a train, maybe reading an article in the newspaper and they put the newspaper down and think about it for several minutes and just allow their body to absorb the information and muse over it and then discuss it later. That's an example of active meditation. And a lot of people think they don't have the ability to meditate, but really most people do because if you just show up somewhere for a spiritual discussion you are in the process of actively meditating over something with other people.

4. Seeking Inspiration

This is the practice is praying for inspiration. . That is when you can either sit down by yourself and get into a relaxed state and ask the universe for ideas or answers, for God's will, for the ability and the strength to do the right thing, and that's what we mean by praying for inspiration or seeking inspiration. One of the truths about inspiration is, you don't have to act on it; you can seek wise counsel about the inspiration that you've received and ask if it's a good idea. Or, you can just run it through a generalized litmus test. Is the idea or is the inspiration something that will help other people, or something that will be unselfish and loving and good for your heart and your mind? Those are things to ask yourself when you seek inspiration and when you decide to act on the inspiration.

5. Seeking God Consciousness

Praying for the presence of the universe and praying for the presence of God. This includes praying for the energy of God and the spirit of the universe to be with you, to be conscious of it, and to cultivate a God-consciousness. Next, you can seek to develop a harmonious relationship with your universe and with your God and to be at peace with yourself, other people, and with nature. Ultimately, if you can ask for all these things and be open to perceiving them, you will actually find that you have developed a consciousness of love of yourself and the world around you. That is the ultimate goal of most orthodox practitioners of spirituality, and that goal is unity and non-separateness, a unity with your authentic self and unity with God and the world.

6. Mass as a Sacrament

Attending a religious service or mass as a sacramental act. What people overlook is many orthodox spiritual practitioners carry out the ritual of attending a temple or a church or a cathedral or some spiritual house. For the people who attend those services and rituals, those activities are a sacrament, a sacred act. Included in many rituals are singing, chanting, and praying, supplicating, and even circumambulating—a word I like to use that means "walking around." It also refers to the ritual movement of people, whether it be a priest, a rabbi, or other religious leader—the movement of people in a sacred space, asking for and invoking the power and presence of the supernatural into that place of worship—that is a sacrament. The circumambulation, the movement, is certainly a part of the spiritual practice, participating in it, being part of it, and seeing it. Many people actually participate in it by either singing or being part of a choir or being part of the group on the altar that does certain things, and they don't have to be priests, they can just be helping out. So, that is actually a very high orthodox practice.

7. Absorption Exercise:

There is a principle called absorption in Mother Nature, and it happens when plants and animals absorb what is around them. They are able to take in the nutrients, food, and sunlight that they need to grow and to be healthy. As human beings and spiritual beings, one of our primary jobs is to learn to absorb the beneficence of the universe, to absorb what is good around us. That includes the sunlight and the trees and the fresh air and the wonderful scents and aromas that we smell in our environment and the sounds and the noises and the animals and the wildlife and the mountains and the beaches to see it, to feel it, to absorb it, to take it in. This is about learning how to pause and take a deep breath and really draw in life's energy, draw in life's energy. The flip side of that is we need to be able to learn to strategically avoid things that rob us of our energy or steal from us without our permission. I know that's not always possible, but we can strategically avoid toxic situations, toxic people, and toxic encounters and avoid escalating situations where the problem can only get worse. Remember that nine out of ten times great miracles can happen when we just walk away and keep our mouth shut, and there is a time and a place for all of us to stand up for ourselves with or against other situations, issues, or people. But in general, and we need to know, you know, when you are in the presence of another person close your eyes and test how you feel around that other person. Are they taking energy from you? Is there a kindred spirit? Do they help you grow? Do they support you? Do they sustain you? This is not only people, but it can be places and things as well.

With this law of absorption you may need to take a few minutes each morning or each evening before you go to bed, close your eyes and take a few deep breaths and relax each part of the body, and then just consciously think to yourself of what is good in the universe, what good happened to you during the day, what blessings happened. Take some time to think about those people who have been good to you over your lifetime and try and feel that goodwill that came to you, feel that love that someone gave to you in the past. It could be your spouse or your aunt or your uncle, your mother, your father or your brother, your sister, or a teacher. Just think of that one person who gave you love and try to be thankful for that in your heart and in your mind. And remember that each day that supply surrounds us, abundance surrounds us—the air, the water, the life. But we must be open in our heart and in our mind to receiving freely of this supply.

8. **Willingness Exercise:**

Practice willingness. What kind of willingness is good and healthy? What kind of willpower is good and healthy? The short answer is that when you decide and allow yourself to do something and you take that first step of action, you become willing by moving in the direction of your ideas and your dreams. But the real tough part of it is that you have to learn to exert your will. In doing so, you draw yourself closer to the abundance of the universe and closer to your GOD. , To be willing you have to be able to persist. You have to believe and accept that your goal is possible. Many writers have said the idea wouldn't even be in your mind if it wasn't possible. For many of us it's just difficult to accept and take life's abundance and reach our hands out and let the gift be put in our hands. One famous author used to begin his presentations by holding up $100 bill and saying, "Who wants $100?" It could be a crowd of 1,000 people and finally after 10 or 20 seconds usually one person would finally jump out of their chair and run up there and grab the money.   That's the way we have to look at life and sometimes we have to just get up and make our move and take what life is offering us and meet life halfway. Meet Mother Nature halfway. Meet your god and your maker and your creator halfway. Meet the spirit of the universe halfway.

9. Give It Away Exercise:

Giving of yourself which builds you up from the inside. Further, we learn things when we teach them. Giving is tangible and intangible and we all benefit if we are able to tithe to others in divinely inspirational ways. We have to be able to give of ourselves the best of ourselves to the universe and the universe will continue to give to us. It doesn't mean you have to donate all your time to charity or donate all of your money to charity, but it does mean that when you are helping others with your spare time or doing the best to support your family and your children, it has a ripple effect on your life and humanity in general. You know, the better you learn to take care of yourself the better you can take care of others. If you learn to take care of your family, you know society will help take care of you.

10. Character Building Ritual

Character building is an exercise in itself. The thing we have to remember is that our character is what creates our vibration, and our vibration is what attracts things to our life. We have to continue to build our character and that means adding things to our lives that are good for us on a body, mind, and spirit level. And we have to improve those things, while letting go of the things that hold us back and keep us down. This means letting go of the bad habits that keep us from heading in the direction of our dreams. So, our character attracts the same type of energy to us just like two tuning forks vibrate at the same level. It's a type of resonance. It's how we radiate our good feelings. If we radiate vibrations of excellence and advancement and improvement, people will be attracted to us. When people sense we are giving more to life than we are taking from it, the want to do business with us or even have relationships with us.

Sometimes I counsel people whose lives are in a rut and they are trying to make some big changes are stuck, and I always tell them to be careful about getting into a relationship at this time. You have a better chance of making life changes if you are not trying to develop a new relationship, and likewise, you will be available for a meaningful relationship once you get your inner house in order. A person who is going to the gym, taking care of their body and going to school, taking care of their mind, or taking on a new job and getting new skills, will become more attractive to other people.

The next thought is just about your purpose. All of us have to find meaning in life, and we have to pick a purpose. We have to dedicate ourselves to something and choose the direction we want to go in. This could be choosing big goals or a five- or ten-year goal, or it could just be a one-day goal. In any event, you have to pick something. You have to commit to different activities. We have to commit to different tasks and goals and we have to find our purpose. Purpose for us is what you above all want to accomplish, either today or for the rest of your life. Maybe you can't figure that out right now, but at least write it down this question: "What do I really, really want to do, dedicate myself to?" Maybe it could be some niche idea or topic of study or research, just what do I want to specialize in, or what do I want to be the best at? Once you find that goal and you are ready to go forward and never look back—that's usually what defines greatness. People who can pick something and stay focused on it can become great in that particular area if they are willing to commit to it and dedicate their lives to it and never look back.

11. **Awareness Exercise:**

Fo us to be aware we need to wake up. We need to wake up in our minds. We need to see truth regardless of appearances and we need to lose our sense of separateness from the world and allow ourselves to be part of it and to see it, to feel it, to interact with it and be more and more aware of our surroundings. When we do this, we can become saturated with the idea that there is abundance and prosperity in this world.

12. **Association Exercise:**

The law of association is the principle that says that we become more like the energies that we association with. The more time you spend with somebody or the more you are in a certain type of environment, the more one you are going to become one with it and the more you are going to identify with a certain group of people, a certain place, or certain types of things.

13. **Creativity:**

All of us are born with a certain creativity, a certain type of expression. We have to learn to express ourselves and express that God-given talent and learn to express it at the highest level we can. It could be little ideas, it could be little bits of creativity, it could be making little pieces of art, writing little poems, creating special clothing, or making little arts and crafts that people want. Every one of us have our own desires to express ourselves and be our authentic selves and express our authentic purpose. What I'm trying to say to you is that unless we head in the direction of our creativity and use our hands and our minds and our bodies we may become frustrated in life that we are not participating in our ideas and our creativeness that belongs to us.

14. **Spiritual Gymnasium**

Mental and spiritual strength are vital to maintain, and I do believe many of us need to continue in the spiritual gymnasium everyday to continue in that prosperity and abundance workout every day. If you can cultivate a prosperity consciousness that becomes so strong that you are easily able to harvest abundance, then you will have developed real spiritual strength. You have to learn to be so strong as to deny and refute the endless possibilities of something not going your way because it's very easy for us to sit around and say, oh, this is going to happen, this bad is going to happen, or this is not going to go my way. It's so easy to be a nega-holic. But by the same token, if you can focus your mind at looking at all of the possibilities of greatness and wealth and abundance and creativity, then you will be immune from the sickness of negativity.

15. Sacred Days

We should observe sacred days, which could include various holidays: Christmas or Easter, St. Joseph's Day, All Saints/Red Mass, 12th Night, or even May Day. Many of these sacred days are based on the lives of Saints, the lives of the masters or, of course, seasonal festivities. Participation in these festivities may call for different rituals, different types of altars, different types of songs, different types of vestments and attire. Some even have a Festival of Saints, for instance, Semana Santa. People in Spain dress up in special outfits and carry large candles and they have different marching groups, and they go through the town. In some of these cities and towns, whether it be Germany or Austria or Span, have these sacred festivals. Some of them are hundreds of years old. They're even in different parts of Germany. They have carnival days which some people call Drei Tolle Tage or Three Crazy Days that goes back almost 800 years as it relates to Carnival Karneval. These are sacred days. These festivities allow people to fellowship and congregate and celebrate certain times of the year. Some people even were able to unwind and relax as a by-product of these festivities. And other types of festivities allow them to enter sacred meditation, sacred prayer, sacred communion with either a spiritual master or holy person like the Mother Mary.

16. Services and Sacred Space

Another type of ritual is praying the stations of the cross, fasting, or even communion itself. In any of these cases, you may be invoking the Spirit of the Universe, God, or Christ, Mother Mary, or some other master and invoking the presence of that master into your life. And you may also engage in certain types of fasting or dietary restrictions as a symbol of sincerity. With communion and during masses and liturgies, the priests are invoking the presence and the actual energy of God into the alter and congregation, and they're administering that sacred energy or communion to individuals to help unite them with the Holy Spirit as well as remove their sins and help protect them from wickedness.

17. Nature Bound and Pilgrimages and Commitments

We can all benefit from the practice of retreat or a time-out or a visit with nature, or even a committed rehabilitation of some sort. There are people who actually take vows with a certain organization perhaps as a monk or an oblate. These are different types of specialized higher rituals with higher degrees of commitment. I've know many families who go on annual retreats together. Some of them are quiet retreats. Some of them are active retreats where they're at a place and eating with others. This type of communal activity is a way to get quiet and relax and get back to the roots of your faith and your life and help draw closer to God and nature. Another example might be a pilgrimage of some sort, such as a hadj or people in Europe that are traveling to a holy place. Some people go to holy places of healing and ask for healing, whether it be in France or Germany or Jerusalem or wherever. In Japan there's these holy places that people go to so they can seek out the energy. Some people refer to these holy places as energy centers. If you've ever been to the top of a pyramid, say in Central America, and felt the energy of that, you would know exactly what I'm talking about. An example of that would be the pyramid in Tepotzlan, Mexico where you can crawl to the top of the mountain. It's a fantastic little way to commune with nature and the heavens. There's actually steps that go up to the top of that mountain.

18. Communing with Yourself

Now another facet of a retreat would be an individualized type of retreat. If you look at the old Celtic, Viking, and Norse literature, there were people there that would go sitting. They would do what is called sitting out and commune with themselves. They invoke the presence of nature and they would seek out the inspiration and guidance of the Fetch, which would be the animal part of their soul. Some people relate most to a lion or a bear or an eagle. You can go out into nature and commune with whatever animal part of your nature that you feel closest to. It's different than the clan part of your soul that they call the Sippe. The Fetch, the part of your animalistic part of your soul, is what some people also consider your guardian angel. Many people consider that they have a guardian angel. In some other cultures, that guardian is believed to be an actual animal itself or that animal part of your soul, which is fascinating. Some people refer to that in mystical books as the elemental body.

So, these are various types of things you can do to commune with yourself and nature and God: retreats, rehabilitation and sitting out, pilgrimages, and taking in nature, or a nature trip. All of these are ways to get closer to God and to yourself and to Earth.

19. Catharsis and Purification

Around the world, regardless of culture and spirituality or tribe, there are groups that form different purification rituals. These rituals could be done when a baby is born or comes of age to be baptized. Purification could be done through either water or submersion into water, or it could be done through the application of an ointment **** or smoke. If you've ever seen Native Americans, sometimes they can smudge a person or blow smoke on them to purify them and their body or purify a room. That's just an example of clearing. In the Celtic and Viking literature you'll see different types of magical clearing of space where they perform clearing of an area. They could clear to the north and the south and the east and the west. The geographical points, of course, were in the upper and the lower, you'll see that in a Native American seven-direction type exercise. So the purification practices are utilized in various cultures globally.

What I find interesting is that in the Ancient East, including India, purification involves two actions: catharsis: cleansing and emptying. However, in the ancient literature, it also included a practice of FILLING, and I think filling is one of the most overlooked aspects of spiritual catharsis which involves cleansing and purification. Let's say you've been through a tough life and you've had some fears and resentments and some angers and some ideas related to the past that you want to let go; there are two ways to do it. You can try to empty yourself and let go of those issues, those ideas and thoughts, but you can also start filling your mind and your heart with new ideas, new affirmations, new decrees, new empowerments, and new ways of thinking. That also leads to new habits and new actions. Our character is about the totality of our thinking and action and omissions, three different areas; but if you are able to develop new thinking and new habits, you can affect your character. So, developing new ideas, forming new beliefs, and forming new habits, that's really a process of magic that changes us at the core of our being. It changes our DNA structure and it changes our neural pathways, all of that is augmented and changed. And even our future is changed as a by-product of it because if you can continue to clear yourself and add only what's good for you and healthy for you into your life, it affects your life moment to moment and into the future as well. Because if you continue to do good things in the moment then many times it has a ripple effect into the future and with what you think each day in the way you wake up each morning.

20. Contemplative Action

Become contemplative in action. That means to become mindful of the universe while you are engaging in life's activities, not only mindful but connected to the energy of the universe. Connected to the positive source, which most people call God, so you're connected and contemplative while in action. You're mindful while you're working, and you're connected to that perfect energy. One of the keys to being mindful is to be more aware while you are connected.

So, you're trying to do the right thing, while also being more aware of your surroundings at any given moment, more aware of what's going on inside you. More aware of what's going on outside of you. With that higher awareness, with that higher connection, you're operating at a higher level, and you're not missing out on the signs and symbols and miracles of life, and the gifts that come to you and the people that are sent to you. All of that is extremely important when remaining contemplative in action. It's like being in a meditative state while being active at the same time.

21. Daily Meditations and Daily Prayers

Daily spiritual ritual including morning and evening prayers and seasonal prayers. Regardless of what faith and spirituality you are there's probably some good books that can help you in developing your daily meditations, your daily prayers, your daily devotions. All of this is there to help you get into the alpha state, get into the meditative state each day, and become connected to your world and become at peace with yourself and other people. Take a few deep breaths and really prepare for your day, and take time in the evening to prepare to go to sleep, and see if you can be a better person in the next day.

Now, a daily ceremony can also mean just a book that you read and meditate over when you're doing your daily prayers. Many people also attend a daily service or an evening or morning mass they could go to with a few people, and that way they're able to pray and commune with each other. They have a little service where they're able to ask for help, and ask for forgiveness, and for empowerment to be of service to the world and to their family.

22.   Meditative Objects

There are many ways to use icons, prayers cards and meditative objects and services. This is very interesting. I don't know if you've ever walked in on a maze, a spiritual maze, and taken the steps according to the actual little walk and made the prayers in each little section of the maze, but that's just an example of a prayer type of activity related to yourself, and to the given place. The other thing is with icons, you may have little icons on your desk or in your home that remind you of a spiritual master or a god or a holy mother or Buddha or whatever it might be. The point of that is just to recognize and be able to have that consciousness or higher power.

Prayer cards are something smaller. Of course, you can keep them in your wallet or in your purse and they may have a beautiful picture on one side and a prayer on the other side. And it's something you can hold and physically look at and pray. If there's a special prayer on one side for protection or whatever, it could be a saint on the card, or it could be Jesus Christ, it could be Lakshmi, the goddess of progeny and abundance from India, it doesn't matter. The point being is that it's a physical object that allows you to stay connected. You're not worshipping the object. You're just using it as a reminder and a mental refresher of your commitment to being spiritually connected. In addition, there are services that are less liturgy oriented, and they're more meditative oriented. If you've ever been to a Taize service, you'll understand that it's a type of meditative service in a regular Christian Church where you try and meditate on an object and an idea in quietude.

23. Spiritual Jewelry and Charms

Another type of personal ritual and practice that many people have is just the collection of spiritual charms to wear whether it be a necklace or a bracelet, or something to hold in your pocket or a keychain, or it could be anything like that or some type of medallion. I'm sure some people may even use an earring or some other type of ring, but that's beside the point. I'm not really talking so much about charms and amulets. I'm mainly talking about reminders, reminders of protection and the power of protection, and the power of blessings that you may want to carry with you or wear on your body.

An example would be the cross of St. Benedict. It's a fantastic cross, and it has the Latin words inscribed up and down the cross that a lot of people don't know, but it says "The cross will protect me that goes before me" on one side of it, and on the other side of the cross it says that "No demon will be able to get me." So, it's kind of a fantastic little charm that goes back probably 300 or more years which is really amazing in one particular faith. And that's just one example of a type of charm or a cross that is carried by certain people.

24. Energy Centers

There are an abundance of holy and sacred places, for example: a Chapel, a Hindu Temple, Pyramid, Cathedral, or a other sacred edifice. For instance, I remember once going to a large place of worship, a citadel in Cairo, and going in there to pray, and it's just a fantastic experience and I did the same in Singapore with a Hindu temple. It doesn't matter where you are around the world. In Latin America, I remember going to say some prayers on the top of a Mayan Pyramid or an Aztec Temple. I later found that this Pyramid was known for its local warrior god of which many people still pray toward today. So, these are just examples of sacred places that many people today call "energy centers" around the world that people like to visit as a sacred pilgrimage of sorts.

25. Higher Self Visitation Exercises

There are vast exercises used to cultivate a relationship with your higher self, and one of the exercises and rituals that I've seen is to commune with yourself in a visual way. You would do a visualization or an enhanced meditation where you see yourself meeting with your higher self in a sacred place to commune.

Communing with yourself is an "inner transformation" or doppelganger type of exercise, because you're meeting with your higher self or your double. To begin this "meet your authentic self" exercise requires your relaxed imagination. Some people may see themselves as a bird or a falcon flying through the sky, through the forest and landing at the sacred place. Then they morph back into their bodies or into a human being who then walks to the sacred door. Upon opening the door they walk into a great hall and see this other self of theirs up on a throne or maybe at the end of a table, and they sit down and talk to that other self. That other self can look like yourself or it can look like another race; it can have long dark hair, long blonde hair, it can have a crown, or it can be a man or a woman, it doesn't matter. It's what you feel your higher self or higher source would look like. It's part of your soul.

You ask that person questions, deep questions, questions you want to answer, maybe advice, and it may give you something deeper and more authentic than even your own wisdom. It may be able to give you calmer and more sincere answers to questions that you are seeking to answer. The answers may even be different or modified in some way than the ones that you've already come up with by yourself. So, it's a fantastic exercise. Or you could just go there to be thankful, and to be safe with this person, and to commune with this other side of yourself, this higher side that is tapped into the source of all energy.

26.   Mantras

Short or memorized prayers can be as simple as a prayer that you've either written by yourself or someone else has written, like the serenity prayer by Reinhold Niebuhr, which is quite famous, or the St. Joseph prayer or any other great prayer. People may use it as a mantra, or just a short prayer that you just may use one word, like God or prosperity or whatever, and you can say this again and again to yourself, silently in meditation or during the course of your day and that's an example of a prayer mantra that you may have.

27. Prayer for Others and Forgiveness

Praying for others is extremely important, and that includes internal and external forgiveness. Many people pray for the welfare of their loved ones or family, their children, their relatives, and so forth, and then there's other types of prayers. You may want to pray for somebody who is a leader or pray for someone you dislike or pray for someone that you want to forgive, whether they're living or not living. People who have gone into group therapy or private therapy may at times send a letter to someone or leave a letter on someone's tomb or even facilitate a rite of penitence.

28. Hospitality Exercise

Another type of spiritual practice or ritual would be just hospitality and this goes back really to the ancient peoples of many cultures, whether it's an Eskimo culture or a German culture or a Russian culture. I'm just giving you some examples. When a stranger comes to your door and they're hungry, that type of hospitality, feeding the individual, the traveler, with food and drink and hospitality and maybe even a place to sleep, all of these things are important. I think maybe today hospitality has been transformed into helping making sure people have a safe place to stay and some healthy food to eat when they're in need. It's very, very important. In its highest form, hospitality honors those who are contributing to humanity and you give or tithe to others to support their good works.

29. Celtic Action

Many Celtic prayers are based in action and activities. There are examples of people who say little prayers along with their actions. They may say a prayer when they do the harvest or a prayer when they serve dinner or a prayer when they kill a beast that will be used to feed the family or the tribe. I'm giving you some shamanic examples, but these are just examples of how specialized prayers are used for everyday activities and everyday events.

30. Sabbath

Having a sacred day during the week is generally know as Sabbath. It could be on Sunday, but in other cultures it may be Friday or a Saturday or another day. Whenever it is, it's having quality time to either take care of yourself or take care of your family members or your children or to commune with nature or to be silent or even in some cultures to commune with your ancestors or those that have gone before you. These are all examples of how the Sabbath is important. Many people attend mass or a church service or a temple or other type of service. So all of this is part of keeping one day special where you can rest and recuperate and be prepared for the rest of your week.

31. Environmental Exercise

The section is about an eco-ritual or environmental harmony that's based on many Shamanic cultures, but particularly some of the pagan cultures of ancient Europe and Asia and in Africa. It involves having environment respect and respect for animals, much like the Native Americans did, and respecting the trees and the plants and the crops and even like I had read a book by Thich Nhat Hanh once and he even talked about it. He's a famous Buddhist Monk and he even talked about how he ate his meals he would sometimes pray while eating or pray before or after eating, pray in thankfulness to all the animals and the trees that worked in harmony to create his food. So, all of us want to keep nature unpolluted and protect our forests and our rivers and our mountains, and environmental respect goes back and is a timeless part of spirituality and respect from the beginnings of time until now in many cultures. Trees and other things have been used, either before Christ or afterwards, in the use of sacraments or rituals.

32. Character Exercise

The section is about precepts or character building and this is about a ritual. Whether you look at Marcus Aurelius or Ben Franklin, or at the present moment people like Steven Covey, you're looking at your daily activities and how you can be a better person each day and maybe you might make a list at the end of the day of the things you did well and the things you didn't do well and see if you can improve on them. In 12-step lingo, the 10th step focuses on being a good person each day and trying to be good to others and make amends to others when you can. Even if you read the writings of Pythagoras or Buddha you would see this same type of character building virtues in their practices, and with Socrates as well, in virtues and ethics in their daily lives.

33. Tithe Exercise

Giving and receiving is part of our world. Generosity and giving are timeless activities based on love and compassion. There are 2 types of giving. 1) giving to those who need help 2) giving to those who are expanding their talents, abilities, and craft. Either type of giving is inherently good. Practice giving your time or money to that which inspires you divinely.

The Process of Magic and Manifesting

1. As beings that desire increasing life, we each contain energies of body, mind and spirit of which we must maintain equilibrium between all three energies. To preserve this balance we utilize our threefold powers. Use of mental, spiritual and physical powers in a spiritual way must produce abundance.
2. All thoughts begin with an idea which is the byproduct of divine connection to the source of all thought.
3. The ideas in back of the thought are the mystical form of all creation and the underpinnings of tangible results or manifestation.
4. All thoughts tend to lead to the field of potential outcomes for all actions, inactions, and creation.
5. Deep Thinking or what is believed in mind habitually becomes who you are and is your essence or character.

6. Free will creates Choices where commitments must be selected. We all have the ability to choose how we use free will in terms of thoughts and actions.
7. Choices create the nucleus of new form and begin a chain reaction if the choice is fueled with emotion and belief.
8. Emotions that fuel manifestation are love, joy, peace, happiness, goodness, and other positive emotions.
9. When each idea is transformed into a intention, then each intention may be transformed into a plan, vision, and mission. Then it is chosen as a prime objective for the individual
10. When the plan is primus it becomes a purpose which is backed by belief.
11. When firm belief, earnestness and constructive emotion are in back of a purpose, it is energized.
12. Our belief system must be based on the constant and creative possibility of optimal results and prosperity. Everyone who is living upright in a spiritual way is deserving and capable of tapping into this abundance.
13. We become best at co-creating our destiny when we are in spiritual unity with the universe where a person develops the realization of the Divine Presence within one's own self.
14. We operate most effectively when we are awakened and clear in mind. Attunement and forgiveness of ourselves and others allows us to be free of anger and to live in the present moment fully in an awakened state of mind.
15. Acceptance - We must believe that prosperity and well-being is our birthright.
16. Believe that you have wealth and freedom and that you are the essence of creative ability.
17. Everything that is needed is continually provided by an ever expanding world and universe that is abundant and impersonal.
18. We must understand the essence or rationale behind the purpose of each desire that we want to cultivate.

19. Further, we must comprehend in some way how our big ideas will help others along with ourselves to convey the sincere impression of value, worth, and increase.
20. Before implementing each plan or taking any big step, we evaluate our mental effectiveness. Getting clear and going thought a catharsis of mind. This means to look at your track record, atone, prune, purge, and clear away the mental debris. Begin to use "what works" and start to utilize the best practices which make you efficient.
21. Clear Objectives - Set specific goals, research and refine them. After the purpose, task and objective is clear, then push forward with persistence.
22. Results Driven. What is the mission, destination, vision. Develop affirmations that correlate to the most favorable end-result.
23. Think, feel and act "AS IF" you are already in possession of the life that you want. Cultivate your emotions and your character around the "As If". You must become what you want which means you become the person who owns the life you desire.
24. Look at where you are, where you are going and periodically reset the course and navigation to optimize the journey.
25. Learn to think and speak in a prosperous way that conveys peace, abundance, and increase. Mold the habits and tendencies of your thought. Refuse to accept lack and fear.
26. Take action. Keep lists and do three things toward your dreams per day, do them constructively to the best of your ability.
27. Study your life, reflect on your day, decide how to continually improve yourself. Do your homework and do all you can to learn and know your purpose, objectives and master your skills. Be the best at what you do and BE Known for your excellence.
28. Meditations and Prayer - Write out affirmative meditations such as, "Each day I am improving". Write out 10 statements that are affirming and positive. Contemplate over them each day. You can write out generalized affirmations or very specific ones.

29. Use the affirmative statements or contemplation, to increase acceptance of our potential and boost our awareness.
30. Visualize - See yourself in optimal circumstances in your mind's eye and Feel it. If you can visualize the optimal result, then see the next step. Example. See yourself a few pounds leaner toward your optimal weight.
31. Choose your environment. Select what to feed yourself. Mold your circumstances by your actions and specific thought.
32. Organize your affairs. Gain the habit of finishing things well. Become excellence, simplify your life, empty the clutter, and redefine your focus. Develop prosperity based routines.
33. Imprint and affirm your ideals and dreams into your consciousness. The plan, desired thing, or result must be written and then verbalized. It should be claimed into this world using the spoken word.
34. Make wealth and excellence a priority. Align your thoughts to attract excellence and wealth. Be aware, be open, learn to receive from others, offer praise, and appreciate life. Accept your potentiality, gifts, and abundance.
35. Circulate your GOOD. Service and Giving - Donate time or money to people or organizations who are the source of your spiritual sustenance.
36. Sixth Sense - Learn and practice creativity, awareness, and contemplation. Keep a journal, write out ideas, develop and allow a universal flow of inspiration and ideas into your life.
37. Review and remember your actions. Reflect on what you have done well each day and things you may not have excelled upon. Be determined to be better and do the right thing. Over 200 years ago, Ben Franklin worked his precepts of order each evening. He wanted to be excellent and build his character even at a mature age.
38. Research ideas - What are your passions, how do your ideas serve? Listen to your intuition & cultivate strategy. Look at what it would take to implement or be successful with your new ideas: then

act on them, implement the plan, review the plan and then improve it.
39. List out streams of income and potential ways to serve and be prosperous. List how you will expand your life. Go past your comfort zones. List goals beyond your expectations and have deadlines of specificity. You can always change the date.
40. Review your lists and projects. Check off your accomplishments.
41. Meet with partners, family and/or spouse to define goals.
42. Discover your natural expression. What is your labor of love. Where do your passions lie. Remember that you work to pay bills, but you should always follow your dreams. Devote 20 percent of your waking hours each week to your passion. If you become great at it, odds are you can earn a living doing it too.
43. Character - How do you want to BE.? Self respect and self regard can be developed and nurtured. When you rebuild yourself, you will in-turn love yourself better which allows you to be kinder, more generous, and more loving to others.
44. With Character comes responsibility toward your mental, physical and spiritual health. Do what works to take care of yourself with: diet, exercise, learning, sleep, study, and fellowship.
45. Associate with those who can help you where you can also help them. Create a network of business and spiritual friends.
46. Be good to your self. Learn health self regard and cultivate a loving relationship with the Source.
47. Teaching others - Giving it away to keep it.
48. Law of Increase and Charisma - Radiate abundance, cheer and enthusiasm. Be contagious with love, cheer, and enthusiasm.

Part III. - Appendix - Confessio Fraternitatis R.C - AD Eruditos Europa

An inkling of the substance of Rosicrucianism--its esoteric doctrines--can be gleaned from an analysis of its shadow--its exoteric writings. In one of the most important of their manifestos, the *Confessio Fraternitatis*, the Brethren of the Fraternity of R.C. seek to justify their existence and explain the purposes and activities of their Order. In its original form the *Confessio* is divided into fourteen chapters, which are here summarized. The Confessio is important as a motivator of the peoples who were oppressed by both politics and religion at the time, however, the manifesto was not a code or doctrine of virtues and spiritual truth. The mysteries and insights were delivered in the lodges and in secret. These mysteries were delivered to BUILD the MAN on a mental, physical, and spiritual level with a distinct focus on CHARACTER and VIRTUE.

Chapter I. Do not through hasty judgment or prejudice misinterpret the statements concerning our Fraternity published in our previous manifesto-- the *Fama Fraternitatis*. The true purpose of our Order was set forth in the Fama Fraternitatis. In this document, we hope so to clarify our position so that you will be moved to join with us in the dissemination of spiritual knowledge according to the secrets of our illustrious brotherhood.

Chapter II. The Rose Croix Fraternity has provided a remedy for the infirmities of the world's philosophic systems. The secret philosophy of the R.C. is founded upon that knowledge which is the sum and head of all faculties, sciences, and arts. By our divinely revealed system--which partakes much of theology and spiritual- mental medicine but little of jurisprudence--we analyze the heavens and the earth; but mostly we study man himself, within whose nature is concealed the supreme secret. If the people of our day accept our invitation and join themselves to our Fraternity, we will reveal to them undreamed-of secrets and wonders concerning the hidden workings of the Universe.

Chapter III. Do not believe that the secrets discussed in this brief document are lightly esteemed by us. We cannot describe fully the marvels of our Fraternity lest the uninformed be overwhelmed by our astonishing declarations and the vulgar ridicule the mysteries which they do not comprehend. We also fear that many will be confused by the unexpected generosity of our proclamation, for not understanding the wonders of this age, they do not realize the great changes which are to come. Like blind men living in a world full of light, they discern only through the sense of feeling. [By *sight* is implied spiritual cognition: by *feeling*, the material senses.]

Chapter IV. Because of the great depth and perfection of our knowledge, those desiring to understand the mysteries of the Fraternity of R. C. cannot attain to that wisdom immediately, but must grow in understanding and knowledge. Therefore, our Fraternity is divided into grades through which each must ascend step by step to the Great Arcanum. Furthermore, those who receive this knowledge shall become masters of all arts and crafts; no secret shall be hidden from them; and all good works of the past, present, and future shall be accessible to them. The whole world shall become as one book and the contradictions of science and theology shall be reconciled. Rejoice, O humanity! for the time has come when God has decreed that the number of our Fraternity shall be increased, a labor that we have joyously undertaken. The right to receive spiritual truth cannot be inherited: it must be evolved within the soul of man himself.

Chapter V. Though we may be accused of indiscretion in offering our treasures so freely --without discriminating between the godly, the wise, the prince, the peasant--we affirm that we have not betrayed our trust. Seekers will find us worldwide.

Chapter VII. Because of the need of brevity, it is enough to say that our Father C.R.C. was born in the year 1378 and departed at the age of 106, leaving to us the labor of spreading the doctrine of philosophic religion to the entire world. Our Fraternity is open to all who sincerely seek for truth; but we publicly warn the false and impious that they cannot betray or injure us, for God has protected our Fraternity, and all who seek to do it harm shall have their evil designs return and destroy them, while the treasures of our Fraternity shall remain untouched, to be used by the Lion in the establishment of his kingdom.

Chapter VII. We declare that God, before the end of the world, shall create a great flood of spiritual light to alleviate the sufferings of humankind. Falsehood and darkness which have crept into the arts, sciences, religions, and governments of humanity--making it difficult for even the wise to discover the path of reality--shall be forever removed and a single standard established, so that all may enjoy the fruitage of truth. We shall not be recognized as those responsible for this change, for people shall say that it is the result of the progressiveness of the age. Great are the reforms about to take place; but we of the Fraternity of R.C. do not arrogate to ourselves the glory for this divine reformation, since many there are, not members of our Fraternity but honest, true and wise men, who by their intelligence and their writings shall hasten its coming. We testify that sooner the stones shall rise up and offer their services than that there shall be any lack of righteous persons to execute the will of God upon earth.

Chapter VIII. That no one may doubt, we declare that God has sent messengers and signs in the heavens, namely, the new stars in *Serpentarius* and *Cygnus*, to show that a great Council of the Elect is to take place. This proves that God reveals in visible nature--for the discerning few--signs and symbols of all things that are coming to pass. God has given man two eyes, two nostrils, and two ears, but only one tongue. Whereas the eyes, the nostrils, and the ears admit the wisdom of Nature into the mind, the tongue alone may give it forth. In various ages there have been illumined ones who have seen, smelt, tasted, or heard the will of God, but it will shortly come to pass that those who have seen, smelt, tasted, or heard shall speak, and truth shall be revealed. Before this revelation of righteousness is possible, however, the world must sleep away the intoxication of her poisoned chalice (filled with the false life of the theological vine) and, opening her heart to virtue and understanding, welcome the rising sun of Truth.

Chapter IX. We have a magic writing, copied from that divine alphabet with which God writes His will upon the face of celestial and terrestrial Nature. With this new language we read God's will for all His creatures, and just as astronomers predict eclipses so we prognosticate the obscurations of the church and how long they shall last. Our language is like unto that of Adam and Enoch before the Fall, and though we understand and can explain our mysteries in this our sacred language, we cannot do so in Latin, a tongue contaminated by the confusion of Babylon.

Chapter X. Although there are still certain powerful persons who oppose and hinder us--because of which we must remain concealed--we exhort those who would become of our Fraternity to study unceasingly the Sacred Scriptures, for such as do this cannot be far from us. We do not mean that the Bible should be continually in the mouth of man, but that he should search for its true and eternal meaning, which is seldom discovered by theologians, scientists, or mathematicians because they are blinded by the opinions of their sects. We bear witness that never since the beginning of the world has there been given to man a more excellent book than the Holy Bible. Blessed is he who possesses it, more blessed he who reads it, most blessed he who understands it, and most godlike he who obeys it.

Chapter XI. We wish the statements we made in the *Fama Fraternitatis* concerning the transmutation of metals and the universal medicine to be lightly understood. While we realize that both these works are attainable by man, we fear that many really great minds may be led away from the true quest of knowledge and understanding if they permit themselves to limit their investigation to the transmutation of metals. When to a man is given power to heal disease, to overcome poverty, and to reach a position of worldly dignity, that man is beset by numerous temptations and unless he possess true knowledge and full understanding he will become a terrible menace to mankind. The alchemist who attains to the art of transmuting base metals can do all manner of evil unless his understanding be as great as his self-created wealth. We therefore affirm that man must first gain knowledge, virtue, and understanding; then all other things may be added unto him. We accuse the Christian Church of the great sin of possessing power and using it unwisely; therefore we prophesy that it shall fall by the weight of its own iniquities and its crown shall be brought to naught.

Chapter XII. In concluding our *Confessio*, we earnestly admonish you to cast aside the worthless books of pseudo-alchemists and philosophers (of whom there are many in our age), who make light of the Holy Trinity and deceive the credulous with meaningless enigmas. One of the greatest of these is a stage player, a man with sufficient ingenuity for imposition. Such men are mingled by the Enemy of human welfare among those who seek to do good, thus making Truth more difficult of discovery. Believe us, Truth is simple and unconcealed, while falsehood is complex, deeply hidden, proud, and its fictitious worldly knowledge, seemingly a glitter with godly luster, is often mistaken for divine wisdom. You that are wise will turn from these false teachings and come to us, who seek not your money but freely offer you our greater treasure. We desire not your goods, but that you should become partakers of our goods. We do not deride parables, but invite you to understand all parables and all secrets. We do not ask you to receive us, but invite you to come unto our kingly houses and palaces, not because of ourselves but because we are so ordered by the Spirit of God, the desire of our most excellent Father C.R.C., and the need of the present moment, which is very great.

Chapter XIII. Now that we have made our position clear that we sincerely confess Christ; disavow the Papacy; devote our lives to true philosophy and worthy living; and daily invite and admit into our Fraternity the worthy of all nations, who thereafter share with us the Light of God: will you not join yourselves with us to the perfection of yourselves, the development of all the arts, and the service of the world? If you will take this step, the treasures of every part of the earth shall be at one time given unto you, and the darkness which envelopes human knowledge and which results in the vanities of material arts and sciences shall be forever dispelled.

Chapter XIV. Again we warn those who are dazzled by the glitter of gold or those who, now upright, might be turned by great riches to a life of idleness and pomp, not to disturb our sacred silence with their clamorings; for though there be a medicine which will cure all diseases and give unto all men wisdom, yet it is against the will of God that men should attain to understanding by any means other than virtue, labor, and integrity. We are not permitted to manifest ourselves to any man except it be by the will of God. Those who believe that they can partake of our spiritual wealth against the will of God or without His sanction will find that they shall sooner lose their lives in seeking us than attain happiness by finding us.

Johann Valentin Andreæ is generally reputed to be the author of the Confessio. It is a much-mooted question, however, whether Andreæ did not permit his name to be used as a pseudonym by Sir Francis Bacon. Apropos of this subject are two extremely significant references occurring in the introduction to that remarkable potpourri, *The Anatomy of Melancholy*. This volume first appeared in 1621 from the pen of Democritus junior, who was afterwards identified as Robert Burton, who, in turn, was a suspected intimate of Sir Francis Bacon. One reference archly suggests that at the time of publishing *The Anatomy of Melancholy* in 1621 the founder of the Fraternity of R.C. was still alive. This statement--concealed from general recognition by its textual involvement--has escaped the notice of most students of Rosicrucianism. In the same work there also appears a short footnote of stupendous import. It contains merely the words: "Job. Valent. Andreas, Lord Verulam." This single line definitely relates Johann Valentin Andreæ to Sir Francis Bacon, who was Lord Verulam, and by its punctuation intimates that they are one and the same individual.

Appendix - The Fraternity of the Rose Cross & Masonic History

WHO were the Rosicrucians? Were they an organization of profound thinkers rebelling against the inquisitional religious and philosophical limitations of their time or were they isolated transcendentalists united only by the similarity of their viewpoints and deductions? Where was the "House of the Holy Spirit, " in which, according to their manifestoes, they met once a year to plan the future activities of their Order? Who was the mysterious person referred to as "Our Illustrious Father and Brother C.R.C."? Did those three letters actually stand for the words "Christian Rosie Cross"? Was Christian Rosencreutz, the supposed author of the *Chymical Nuptials*, the same person who with three others founded "The Society of the Rose Cross"?

What relationship existed between Rosicrucianism and mediæval Freemasonry? Why were the destinies of these two organizations so closely interwoven? Is the "Brotherhood of the Rose Cross" the much-sought-after link connecting the Freemasonry of the Middle Ages with the symbolism and mysticism of antiquity, and are its secrets being perpetuated by modern Masonry? Did the original Rosicrucian Order disintegrate in the latter part of the eighteenth century, or does the Society still exist as an organization, maintaining the same secrecy for which it was originally famous? What was the true purpose for which the "Brotherhood of the Rose Cross" was formed? Were the Rosicrucians a religious and philosophic brotherhood, as they claimed to be, or were their avowed tenets a blind to conceal the true object of the Fraternity, which possibly was the political control of Europe? These are some of the problems involved in the study of Rosicrucianism.

There are several distinct theories regarding the Rosicrucian origins. Each is the result of a careful consideration of the evidence by scholars who have spent their lives ransacking the archives of Hermetic lore. The conclusions reached demonstrate clearly the inadequacy of the records available concerning the genesis and early activities of the "Brethren of the Rose Cross."

ARMS OF THE MASONS
GERMAN
from an old drawing
A.D. 1565
(Reichsdorff)

The Historical Postulate of Rosicrucianism

Those Fraternal brethren who have investigated the subject accept the historical existence of the "Brotherhood of the Rose Cross" but are divided concerning the origin of the Order. One group holds the society originated in mediæval Europe as an outgrowth of alchemical speculation. Robert Macoy, 33°, believes that Johann Valentin Andreæ, a German theologian, was the true founder, and he also believes it possible that this movement merely reformed and amplified an existing society which had been founded by Sir Henry Cornelius Agrippa. Some believe that Rosicrucianism represented the first European invasion of Buddhist and Brahmin culture. Still others hold the opinion that the "Society of the Rose Cross" was founded in Egypt during the philosophic supremacy of that empire, and that it also perpetuated the Mysteries of ancient Persia and Chaldea.

In his *Anacalypsis*, Godfrey Higgins writes: "The Rosicrucians of Germany are quite ignorant of their origin; but, by tradition, they suppose themselves descendants of the ancient Egyptians, Chaldeans, Magi, and Gymnosophists." (The last was a name given by the followers of Alexander the Great to a caste of naked Wise Men whom they found meditating along the river banks in India.) The consensus among these factions is that the story of Father C.R.C., like the Masonic legend of Hiram Abiff, is an allegory and should not be considered literally. A similar problem has confronted students of the Bible, who have found not only difficult, but in the majority of cases impossible, their efforts to substantiate the historical interpretation of the Scriptures.

Admitting the existence of the Rosicrucians as a secret society with both philosophic and political ends, it is remarkable that an organization with members in all parts of Europe could maintain absolute secrecy throughout the centuries. Nevertheless, the "Brothers of the Rose Cross" were apparently able to accomplish this. A great number of scholars and philosophers, among them Sir Francis Bacon and Wolfgang von Goethe, have been suspected of affiliation with the Order, but their connection has not been established to the satisfaction of prosaic historians. Pseudo-Rosicrucians abounded, but the true members of the "Ancient and Secret

Order of The Unknown Philosophers" have successfully lived up to their name; to this day they remain unknown.

During the Middle Ages a number of tracts appeared, purporting to be from the pens of Rosicrucians. Many of them, however, were spurious, being issued for their self-aggrandizement by unscrupulous persons who used the revered and magic name Rosicrucian in the hope of gaining religious or political power. This has greatly complicated the work of investigating the Society. One group of pseudo-Rosicrucians went so far as to supply its members with a black cord by which they were to know each other, and warned them that if they broke their vow of secrecy the cord would be used to strangle them. Few of the principles of Rosicrucianism have been preserved in literature, for the original Fraternity published only fragmentary accounts of its principles and activities.

In his *Secret Symbols of the Rosicrucians*, Dr. Franz Hartmann describes the Fraternity as "A secret society of men possessing superhuman--if not supernatural--powers; they were said to be able to prophesy future events, to penetrate into the deepest mysteries of Nature, to transform Iron, Copper, Lead, or Mercury into Gold, to prepare an *Elixir of Life*, or *Universal Panacea*, by the use of which they could preserve their youth and manhood; and moreover it was believed that they could command the *Elemental Spirits of Nature*, and knew the secret of the *Philosopher's Stone*, a substance which rendered him who possessed it all-powerful, immortal, and supremely wise."

The same author further defines a Rosicrucian as "A person who by the process of spiritual awakening has attained a *practical knowledge* of the secret significance of the *Rose* and the *Cross.* * * * To call a person a Rosicrucian does not make him one, nor does the act of calling a person a Christian make him a Christ. The real Rosicrucian or Mason cannot be made; he must grow to be one by the expansion and unfoldment of the divine power within his own heart. The inattention to this truth is the cause that many churches and secret societies are far from being that which their names express." The symbolic principles of Rosicrucianism are so profound that even today they are little appreciated. Their charts and diagrams are concerned with weighty cosmic principles which they treat with a philosophic understanding decidedly refreshing when compared with the orthodox narrowness prevalent in their day. According to the available records, the Rosicrucians were bound together by mutual aspirations rather than by the laws of a fraternity. The "Brothers of the Rose Cross" are believed to have lived unobtrusively, laboring industriously in trades and professions, disclosing their secret affiliation to no one--in many cases not even to their own families. After the death of C.R.C., most of the Brethren apparently had no central meeting place. Whatever initiatory ritual the Order possessed was so closely guarded that it has never been revealed. Doubtless it was couched in chemical terminology.

Many suspect the Rosicrucian rose to be a conventionalization of the Egyptian and Hindu lotus blossom, with the same symbolic meaning as this more ancient symbol. The *Divine Comedy* stamps Dante Alighieri as being familiar with the theory of Rosicrucianism. Concerning this point, Albert Pike in his *Morals and Dogma* makes this significant statement: "His Hell is but a negative Purgatory. His heaven is composed of a series of Kabalistic circles, divided by a cross, like the Pantacle of Ezekiel. In the center of this cross blooms a rose, and we see the symbol of the Adepts of the Rose-Croix for the first time publicly expounded and almost categorically explained."

Doubt has always existed as to whether the name Rosicrucian came from the symbol of the rose and cross, or whether this was merely a blind to deceive the uninformed and further conceal the true meaning of the Order. Godfrey Higgins believes that the word *Rosicrucian* is not derived from the flower but from the word *Ros,* which means dew. It is also interesting to note that the word *Ras* means wisdom, while *Rus* is translated concealment. Doubtless all of these meanings have contributed to Rosicrucian symbolism.

A. E. Waite holds with Godfrey Higgins that the process of forming the Philosopher's Stone with the aid of dew is the secret concealed within the name Rosicrucian. It is possible that the dew referred to is a mysterious substance within the human brain, closely resembling the description given by alchemists of the dew which, falling from heaven, redeemed the earth. The cross is symbolic of the human body, and the two symbols together-- the rose on the cross--signify that the soul of man is crucified upon the body, where it is held by three nails.

It is probable that Rosicrucian symbolism is a perpetuation of the secret tenets of the Egyptian Hermes, and that the Society of Unknown Philosophers is the true link connecting modern Masonry, with its mass of symbols, to ancient Egyptian Hermeticism, the source of that symbolism. In his *Doctrine and Literature of the Kabalah*, A. E. Waite makes this important observation: "There are certain indications which point to a possible connection between Masonry and Rosicrucianism, and this, if admitted, would constitute the first link in its connection with the past. The evidence is, however, inconclusive, or at least unextricated. Freemasonry per se, in spite of the affinity with mysticism which I have just mentioned, has never exhibited any mystic character, nor has it a clear notion how it came by its symbols."

Many of those connected with the development of Freemasonry were suspected of being Rosicrucians; some, as in the case of Robert Fludd, even wrote defenses of this organization. Frank C. Higgins, a modern Masonic symbolist, writes: "Doctor Ashmole, a member of this fraternity [Rosicrucian], is revered by Masons as one of the founders of the first Grand Lodge in London." (See *Ancient Freemasonry*.) Elias Ashmole is but one of many intellectual links connecting Rosicrucianism with the genesis of Freemasonry.

The *Encyclopædia Britannica* notes that Elias Ashmole was initiated into the Freemasonic Order in 1646, and further states that he was "the first gentleman, or amateur, to be 'accepted'." On this same subject, Papus, in his *Tarot of the Bohemians*, has written: "We must not forger that the Rosicrucians were the Initiators of Leibnitz, and the founders of actual Freemasonry through Ashmole." If the founders of Freemasonry were initiated into the Great Arcanum of Egypt--and the symbolism of modern Masonry would indicate that such was the case--then it is reasonable to suppose that they secured their information from a society whose existence they admitted and which was duly qualified to teach them these symbols and allegories. One theory concerning the two Orders is to the effect that Freemasonry was an outgrowth of Rosicrucianism; in other words, that the "Unknown Philosophers" became known through an organization which they created to serve them in the material world. The story goes on to relate that the Rosicrucian adepts became dissatisfied with their progeny and silently withdrew from the Masonic hierarchy, leaving behind their symbolism and allegories, but carrying away the keys by which the locked symbols could be made to give tip their secret meanings. Speculators have gone so far as to state that, in their opinion, modern Freemasonry has completely absorbed Rosicrucianism and succeeded it as the world's greatest secret society.

Other minds of equal learning declare that the Rosicrucian Brotherhood still exists, preserving its individuality as the result of having withdrawn from the Masonic Order. According to a widely accepted tradition, the headquarters of the Rosicrucian Order is near Carlsbad, in Austria (see Doctor Franz Hartmann). Another version has it that a mysterious school, resembling in general principles the Rosicrucian Fraternity, which calls itself "The Bohemian Brothers," still maintains its individuality in the *Schwarzwald* (Black Forest) of Germany. One thing is certain: with the rise of Freemasonry, the Rosicrucian Order in Europe practically disappeared, and notwithstanding existing statements to the contrary, it is certain that the 18th degree (commonly known as the Rose-Croix) perpetuates many of the symbols of the Rosicrucian Fire Alchemists.

In an anonymous unpublished manuscript of the eighteenth century bearing the earmarks of Rosicrucian Qabbalism appears this statement: "Yet will I now give the over-wise world a paradox to be solved, namely, that some illuminated men have undertaken to found Schools of Wisdom in Europe and these for some peculiar reason have called themselves *Fratres Rosa: Crucis*. But soon afterwards came false schools into existence and corrupted the good intentions of these wise men. Therefore, the Order no longer exists as most people would understand existence, and as this Fraternity of the *Seculo Fili* call themselves *Brothers of the Rosie Cross*, so also will they in the *Seculo Spiritus Sancti* call themselves *Brothers of the Lily Cross* and the *Knights of the White Lion*. Then will the Schools of Wisdom begin again to blossom, but why the first one chose their name and why the others shall also choose theirs, only those can solve who have understanding grounded in Nature."

The rose is a symbol associated with generation, fecundity, and purity. The fact that flowers blossom by unfolding has caused them to be chosen as symbolic of spiritual unfoldment. The red color of the rose refers to the blood of Christ, and the golden heart concealed within the midst of the flower corresponds to the spiritual gold concealed within the human nature. The number of its petals being ten is also a subtle reminder of the perfect Pythagorean number. The rose symbolizes the heart, and the heart has always been accepted by Christians as emblematic of the virtues of love and compassion, as well as of the nature of Christ--the personification of these virtues. The rose as a religious emblem is of great antiquity. It was accepted by the Greeks as the symbol of the sunrise, or of the coming of dawn. In his Metamorphosis, or Golden Ass, Apuleius, turned into a donkey because of his foolishness, regained his human shape by eating a sacred rose given to him by the Egyptian priests. The presence of a hieroglyphic rose upon the escutcheon of Martin Luther has been the basis of much speculation as to whether any connection existed between his Reformation and the secret activities of the Rose Cross. Political aspirations of the Rosicrucians were expressed through the activities of Sir Francis Bacon, the Comte de St.-Germain, and the Comte di Cagliostro. The last named is suspected of having been an emissary of the Knights Templars, a society deeply involved in transcendentalism, as Eliphas Levi has noted. There is a popular supposition to the effect that the Rosicrucians were at least partial instigators of the French Revolution.

(Note particularly the introduction to Lord Bulwer-Lytton's Rosicrucian novel *Zanoni*.) "The Gnostic sects, the Oriental Christian Mystics, the Arabs, Alchemists, Templars, Rosicrucians, and lastly the Freemasons, form the Western chain in the transmission of occult science." (See *The Tarot of the Bohemians* translated by A. E. Waite from the French of Papus.)

Max Heindel, the Christian mystic, described the Rosicrucian Temple as an "etheric structure" located in and around the home of a European country gentleman. He believed that this invisible building would ultimately be moved to the American continent. Mr. Heindel referred to the Rosicrucian Initiates as so advanced in the science of life that "death had forgotten them."

Origins of The Ancient Esoteric Tradition - Earliest Indo-European Religions

The most ancient world religions of Mesopotamia which include Sumeria, Assyria, and Babylon are built on mythological deities, but also contain the primary wisdom of the warrior way, philosophy, creation myth, law and ethics. To begin with, it is clear that there were commandments or written codes of law by the kings of Mesopotamia. From about 2100 BC which is over 4100 years ago, The Code of Ur-Nammu is the oldest known tablet containing a law code surviving today, and it was written in the Sumerian language. Further, Hammurabi 1810 BC – 1750 BC), who became the first king of the Babylonian Empire, extending Babylon's control over Mesopotamia by winning a series of wars against neighboring kingdoms. From his reign, the code of Hammurabi was created and contained 282 laws, written by scribes on 12 tablets and dated 1780 BC. In perspective, the Great Abraham is said to have lived in the time of 2000 BC (probably under the rule of the Kings of Mesopotamia of this time. It is currently the year 6758 according to the Assyrian calendar of 2008.

Stele of Naram-Sin, (2240 BC) Sargon's grandson, celebrating his victory against the Lullubi from Zagros. with Horned War Helmet and long beard.

Mesopotamian religious views are probably the first in recorded history, and Mesopotamians are said to have believed that the universe or world was a flat disc, surrounded by a huge, holed space, and above that, heaven. Mesopotamians also believed that water was everywhere and that the universe was born from this enormous sea. In addition, Mesopotamian religion was both Henotheistic and polytheistic. This means that Mesopotamians had many gods but Enlil was the most powerful chief God. Although the beliefs described above were held in common among Mesopotamians, there were also regional variations. For example, Sumer was the first civilization of record in Southern Iraq or Mesopotamia. The Sumerian word for universe is An-Ki, which refers to the god An and the goddess Ki. It is quite interesting that the Universe is a combination of masculine and feminine. Sumer is widely considered to be the earliest settled society in the world to have manifested all the features needed to qualify fully as a civilization, dating back approximately 7000 years ago.

In Sumerian mythology, **Eridu** may have been one of the cities built before the great flood and the earliest Sumerian settlement, founded ca.

4,900 BCE, close to the Persian Gulf and Basra near the mouth of the Euphrates River. The son of the Major Gods An and Ki was named Enlil who was the air god. Mesopotamians may have believed that Enlil was the most powerful god and the chief god of the Pantheon, much like the Greeks had Zeus. The gods were said to have created humans from clay for the purpose of serving them. Moreover, in the time around 3000 BC, the later civilizations and mysteries of Egypt would also become prominent.

The 20th century BC Akkadian written work called the **Atra-Hasis** which is named after its human hero, contains both a creation myth and a flood story. It may be one of history's earliest writings. Tablet I contains a creation myth of the Sumerian gods Anu, Enlil and Enki, gods of sky, wind and water. Tablet II has tales of the god Enlil sending famine and drought at intervals of every 1200 years to reduce the population. Tablet III of the Atrahasis Epic contains the flood story. This is the section that was adapted in the Epic of Gilgamesh which was probably written well over 4000 years ago. [xliii]

In a similar way, Greek awareness during the Hellenic era of Osiris had grown, and attempts had been made to merge Greek philosophy, such as Platonism, and the cult of Osiris (especially the myth of his resurrection), resulting in a new mystery religion. Today, the term Osiris-Dionysus is used by some metaphysical teachers of philosophy and spirituality to refer to a group of deities worshipped around the Mediterranean in the hundreds if not thousands of years before the emergence of Christ. Osiris is one of the oldest gods for whom records have been found; one of the oldest known attestations of his name is on the Palermo Stone of around 2500 BC. Isis is the wife of Osiris while Horus being considered his posthumously begotten son It has been posited that all of these deities were closely related in fact and myth and shared many characteristics, most notably being male, partly-human, born of virgins, life-death-rebirth deities and other similar characteristics.

With the above mythology, cosmology, and creation stories, it is easy to see how the Western Metaphysicians are drawn to the historical lessons and stories of the Ancient cultures and mystics of: Mesopotamia, Babylon, Sumeria, Assyria, Egypt, Greece, Persia, Rome, India, Celtic, and others.

Some Core Historical Spiritual Practices and Beliefs of Mesopotamia

- Many gods/saints and powerful deities, but generally revering one MOST powerful God.
- Laws and Ethics for the People (Commandments and Codes)
- Incantation and prayers offered to the God or Gods
- Astrology and use of the stars and heavens for speculation, health, and action.
- Festival Days and Cult worship of the primal Gods
- Sacrifices or gifts to praise the Gods which in turn would feed the attendees.
- Atonement to the Gods
- Building Shrines for Gods – ritual temples called **Ziggurats**.
- The Heart was the center of emotion and reason
- That the spirit or soul was eternal.
- Talismans or Spiritual Symbols used to reinforce mental/spiritual connection.
- Magic and Prayer (invocations, amulets, affirmations)
- Ancestor veneration or reverence
- Purification and cleansing rituals for purity of mind, spirit, or body.

God Ashur or Shamash with Long Hair and Beard encircled by Winged Disc. Ashur and Marduk were worshipped some 3500 years ago after Hammurabi

Babylonian "Counsels of Wisdom" 1500 B.C.

These ancient teachings have been used by scholars to show the wisdom of the ages that preceded the Old Testament. It is highly probable that these teachings were called the, "Instructions of Shuruppak. [xliv]

Other important teachings in this codex are:

- Worship
- Offerings
- Prayer Supplication
- Reverence
- Sacrifice
- Right Speech
- Right Learning & Study
- Praise Others
- Avoidance of bad companions.
- Improper speech.
- Avoidance of altercations and pacification of enemies.
- Kindness to those in need.
- The duties and benefits of religion..
- Improper deception of friends.
- Atonement and mental harmony
- Supplication and Praise toward Good

Notice the 6 Point Star Encircled by the Crescent Moon. Further, there is a six pointed Cross behind the Star. [xlv]

The Stele of Ur-Nammu of Ur 2100BC, who waters the Tree of Life before Shamash the Sun God.

Disclaimer: All Rights Reserved for All Original or Enhanced content herein. Note: Excerpts and chapters have been taken from some of the writers listed in the endnotes. All direct usage is based on content, writings, and images that are in the public domain or pre-1925 information. It was the intent of the editor and author to utilize the best writings, quotes, and insights from the recent past to present the updated and expanded lessons from the 1763-4 Orleans Rites of the Loge de Parfaits de Escosse ™. Terms: All readers agree to practice these teachings in a safe environment. All readers are by implied consent agreeing to seek the help of a qualified and licensed professional for any special psychological or medical needs.

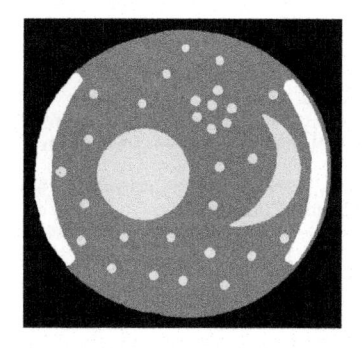

i The Secret Teachings of All the Ages by Manly P. Hall, 1928, copyright not renewed , San Francisco Printed for Manly P Hall by HS Crocker Copany, Inc. MCMXXVIII
http://www.sacred-texts.com/eso/sta/sta34.htm
ii Alan Ax elrod, 1997, Checkmark Books, The International Encyclopedia of Secret Societies and Fraternal Orders. Pg. 212.
iii Yates, Frances A. (1972), The Rosicrucian Enlightnment, London & Edighoffer, Roland (I-1982, II-1987)
iv The Poetic Edda, translation: Henry Adams Bellows, 1936
v Laws of Success – Magus Incognito, Beals
vi **Magus Incognito and Incognito**
vii See: The Rosicrucian Mysteries: An Elementary Exposition of Their Secret Teachings - Page 170 by Max Heindel - Rosicrucians - 1916 - 198 pages
viii W. D. Wattles enhanced by Prof. Incognito from "Financial Success Through Creative Thought " 1910
ix Faivre "Western Hermeticism and the Concept of Western Esotericism" from Gnosis and Hermeticism: from Antiquity to Modern Times pp. 109-10
x Isaac Newton – Emerald Tablet
xi The Secret Doctrine of The Rosicrucians, Magus Incognito, Advanced Thought Publishing, 1918
xii **Magus Incognito 21st Centruy**
xiii Fundamental Laws: A Report of the 68th Convocation of the Rose Cross Order ... - Page 89 by Rose Cross Order, Rose Cross Order - 1916 - 208 pages
xiv How the Mind Works - Page 71 by Dr. Christian D. Larson - New Thought - 1912 - 199 pages
xv How the Mind Works - Page 71by Dr. Christian D. Larson - New Thought - 1912 - 199 pages
xvi The Science of Being Great" by Wattles – Elizabeth Towne Publishing 1914
xvii W. D. Wattles enhanced by Prof. Incognito from "Financial Success Through Creative Thought " 1910
xviii How the Mind Works - Page 71 by Dr. Christian D. Larson - New Thought - 1912 - 199 pages
xix W. D. Wattles enhanced by Prof. Incognito from "Financial Success Through Creative Thought " 1910
xx R. Swinburne Clymer, M.D. (Supreme Grand Master of the Order, Temple, Brotherhood and Fraternity of the Rosicrucians, and of La Federation Universelle des Ordres, del Societes et Fraternite des Initie - "Book of Rosicrucae", 1947, Volume 2, pages 117-118
xxi Mark Skousen . The Compleated Autobiography by Benjamin Franklin (2005)
xxii The Science of Being Great" by Wattles – Elizabeth Towne Publishing 1914
xxiii Joseph Weed - http://arosicrucianspeaks.com/soshall.htm
xxiv G. Behrend & Troward enhanced by Incognito - http://newthoughtlibrary.com/behrendGenevieve/bio_behrend.htm
xxv W.D. Wattles - IBID
xxvi Incognito – Essays on Success 2007
xxvii W.D. Wattles - IBID
xxviii W.D. Wattles – IBID
xxix The Secret Of Success By William Walker Atkinson 1907
xxx W.D. Wattles - IBID
xxxi *Wallace D. Wattles (1910) – Enhanced by Prof. Incognito*
xxxii W. D. Wattles enhanced by Prof. Incognito from "Financial Success Through Creative Thought " 1910
xxxiii William Walker Atkinson. *Thought Vibration or the Law of Attraction.* Advanced Thought Publishing. 1906
xxxiv Lindow, John. *Norse Mythology: A Guide to the Gods, Heroes, Rituals, and Beliefs* (2001) Oxford: Oxford University Press. ISBN 0-19-515382-0.
xxxv Bogoda, Robert (1994). *A Simple Guide to Life* (Wheel No. 397/398). Kandy: BPS. Retrieved 2008-02-04 from "Access to Insight" (1996)
xxxvi *The Historic Note-book: With an Appendix of Battle; By Ebenezer Cobham Brewer, pg. 859*
xxxvii W. D. Wattles enhanced by Prof. Incognito - from "Financial Success Through Creative Thought".
xxxviii **By: Dr. G. S. Incognito, JD, MBA, DSS – Essays**

xl Supreme Magus -Essays and Commentary on Dr. Haanel
xli **Supreme Magus - Commentary**
xlii Selby, Jon and Selig, Zachary. (1992) Kundalini Awakening, a Gentle Guide to Chakra Activation and Spiritual Growth, New York: Random House
xliii George, Andrew R., trans. & edit. (2003). *The Babylonian Gilgamesh Epic: Critical Edition and Cuneiform Texts.* England: Oxford University Press.

[xliv] Lambert, Babylonian Wisdom Literature, (Winona Lake, Indiana: Eisenbrauns, 1996), 1., Lambert considers these in chapter 4,"Precepts and Admonitions," BWL 92-107.

Bibliography:

Black Elk, N. and Neihardt, J. G. (2000) Black Elk Speaks, Lincoln: University of Nebraska Press.

Capra, F. (1989) The Tao of Physics: An Exploration of the Parallels between Modern Physics and Eastern Mysticism, London: Flamingo

Cleary, T. (1992) The Essential Tao: An Initiation in the Heart of Taoism through the Authentic Tao Te Ching and the Inner Teachings of ChuangTzu, New Jersey: Castle Books.

Collier, R. (1999) The Secret of the Ages, Oak Harbor, WA: Robert Collier Publications

Covey, S. R. (1989) The 7 Habits of Highly Effective People, London: Simon & Schuster.

Drury, Nevill. The Elements of Shamanism. Rockport, Mass.: Element Books, 1989.

Eason, Cassandra. The Handbook of Ancient Wisdom. New York: Sterling Publishing, 1997.

Muhammad Al-Ghazzali (1909) The Alchemy of Happiness, trans. Claud Field, London: J. Murray; also at www.sacred-texts.com.

Goleman, D. (1998) Working with Emotional Intelligence, London: Bloomsbury.

Goodwin, Joscelyn. Mystery Religions In The Ancient World. San Francisco: Harper and Row, 1981

Grimm, Jacob. Teutonic Mythology. 4 vols. New York: Dover, 1966.

Franklin, B. (1993) "The Way to Wealth" in Benjamin Franklin: Autobiography and Other Writings, O. Seavey (ed.), Oxford: Oxford University Press.

Heisler, Roger. Path To Power, It's All In Your Mind. York Beach, Maine: Samuel Weiser, 1990

Heschel, A. J. (1975) The Sabbath: Its Meaning for Modern Man, New York: Farrar, Straus and Giroux.

Hill, N. & Stone, W. C. (1990) Success through a Positive Mental Attitude, London: Thorsons.

Hill, N. (1960) Think and Grow Rich, New York: Fawcett Crest.

Hollander, Lee M., trans. The Poetic Edda. 2d ed. Austin: University of Texas Press, 1962.

Jones, Gwyn. A History of the Vikings. London: OxfordUniversity Press, 1973

Jung, C. G. (1978) Memories, Dreams, Reflections, Glasgow: William Collins. The Book of Margery Kempe (1936) trans. W. Butler-Bowdon, London: Jonathan Cape.

Krishnamurti, J. (1970) Think on These Things, New York: Harper & Row.
MacGregor-Mathers, S. L., trans. The Book of the Sacred Magic of Abra-Melin the Mage. Chicago: de Laurence, 1932.
Meyer, Marvin W. The Ancient Mysteries: A Source Book. San Francisco: Harper and Row, 1987
O'Donohue, J. (1998) Anam Cara: Spiritual Wisdom from the Celtic World, London: Bantam.
Pirsig, R. M. (1999) Zen and the Art of Motorcycle Maintenance, London: Vintage.
Redfield, J. (1993) The Celestine Prophecy: An Adventure, New York: Bantam.
Schucman, H. & Thetford, W. (1996) A Course in Miracles, New York: Viking
Scovel Shinn, F. (1978) The Secret Door to Success, Camarillo, CA: De Vorss & Co.
Storms, G. Anglo-Saxon Magic. The Hague: Nijhoff, 1948.
Sun Tzu (2002) The Art of War, Denma Translation Group, Boston: Shambhala.
Suzuki, S. (2003) Zen Mind, Beginner's Mind: Informal Talks on Zen Meditation and Practice, New York: Weatherhill, Inc.
Swedenborg, E. (1976) Heaven and Hell, trans. George F. Dole, New York: Swedenborg Foundation.
Teresa of Avila (1989) Interior Castle, New York: Doubleday.
Tolle, E. (2001) The Power of Now: A Guide to Spiritual Enlightenment, Sydney: Hodder.
Tracy, B. (1993) Maximum Achievement: Strategies and Skills that Will Unlock Your Hidden Powers to Succeed, New York: Fireside.
Turville-Petre, E. O. G. Myth and Religion of the North. New York: Holt, Rinehart and Winston, 1964.
Warren, R. (2002) The Purpose-Driven Life, Grand Rapids: Zondervan.
Wiseman, R. (2003) The Luck Factor: Change Your Luck—And Change Your Life, London: Century.
Ziglar, Z. (2000) See You at the Top: 25th Anniversary Edition, Gretna, LA: Pelican Publishing.

Printed in Dunstable, United Kingdom